OXFORD WORLD'S CLASSICS

THE PRINCE

NICCOLÒ MACHIAVELLI was born in Florence in 1469. Very little is known of his life until his entrance into the Florentine Chancery in 1498, where he served his mentor, the Florentine Standard-bearer Piero Soderini, until the return of the Medici in 1512 overthrew Soderini's republic and caused Machiavelli both the loss of his position and even brief imprisonment for his republican sympathies. *The Prince* was written in 1513 but not published until after Machiavelli's death, in 1532. It has since become a classic of political theory and social thought. In addition to a longer and more complicated work on republics, *Discourses on Livy*, Machiavelli wrote *The Art of War*, *The History of Florence*, lyric poetry, a novella, a number of brief essays and diplomatic narratives, and several plays, including the masterpiece of Italian Renaissance comedy, *The Mandrake Root*. He died in 1527.

PETER BONDANELLA is Distinguished Professor of Comparative Literature and Italian at Indiana University. Past President of the American Association for Italian Studies, he is the author of many books, editions, and translations devoted to Italian literature and cinema, including *Italian Cinema: From Neorealism to the Present* (2002), and *The Cambridge Companion to the Italian Novel* (2003). For Oxford World's Classics he has translated Machiavelli's *Discourses on Livy*, Cellini's *My Life*, and Vasari's *Lives of the Artists*.

MAURIZIO VIROLI is Professor of Politics at Princeton University. His many books include *For Love of Country: An Essay on Patriotism and Nationalism* (1995), *Machiavelli* (1998), *Niccolò's Smile: A Biography of Machiavelli* (1998/2001), and *The Idea of the Republic* (with Norberto Bobbio, 2003).

OXFORD WORLD'S CLASSICS

*For over 100 years Oxford World's Classics have brought
readers closer to the world's great literature. Now with over 700
titles—from the 4,000-year-old myths of Mesopotamia to the
twentieth century's greatest novels—the series makes available
lesser-known as well as celebrated writing.*

*The pocket-sized hardbacks of the early years contained
introductions by Virginia Woolf, T. S. Eliot, Graham Greene,
and other literary figures which enriched the experience of reading.
Today the series is recognized for its fine scholarship and
reliability in texts that span world literature, drama and poetry,
religion, philosophy and politics. Each edition includes perceptive
commentary and essential background information to meet the
changing needs of readers.*

OXFORD WORLD'S CLASSICS

NICCOLÒ MACHIAVELLI

The Prince

Translated and Edited by
PETER BONDANELLA

With an Introduction by
MAURIZIO VIROLI

OXFORD
UNIVERSITY PRESS

OXFORD

UNIVERSITY PRESS

Great Clarendon Street, Oxford OX2 6DP

Oxford University Press is a department of the University of Oxford.
It furthers the University's objective of excellence in research, scholarship,
and education by publishing worldwide in

Oxford New York

Auckland Cape Town Dar es Salaam Hong Kong Karachi Kuala Lumpur
Madrid Melbourne Mexico City Nairobi New Delhi Shanghai Taipei Toronto

With offices in

Argentina Austria Brazil Chile Czech Republic France Greece
Guatemala Hungary Italy Japan South Korea Poland Portugal
Singapore Switzerland Thailand Turkey Ukraine Vietnam

Oxford is a registered trademark of Oxford University Press
in the UK and in certain other countries

Published in the United States
by Oxford University Press Inc., New York

Translation, Explanatory Notes, Select Bibliography © Peter Bondanella 2005
Introduction © Maurizio Viroli 2005

The moral rights of the author have been asserted
Database right Oxford University Press (maker)
Reissued 2008

British Library Cataloguing in Publication Data

Data available

ISBN 978-0-19-953569-9

19

Typeset in Ehrhardt
by RefineCatch Limited, Bungay, Suffolk
Printed in Great Britain by
Clays Ltd, Elcograf S.p.A.

CONTENTS

INTRODUCTION

The Prince has generated polemical discussion ever since its
appearance in the early sixteenth century. This slim volume has
become a classic of modern social thought and a mainstay of
courses on the great books, political theory, and Renaissance culture—and in all of these areas it continues to stimulate heated
debate and controversy. While Machiavelli no doubt expected the
critical tone of his treatise to provoke a sharp response among his
readers, he might well have been surprised by the wide variety of
different interpretations which have been suggested in the course
of the last five centuries. The immediate practical purpose of *The
Prince* was superseded within a decade of its composition, but its
radically original treatment of crucial philosophical and political
issues continues to attract new readers, many of whom are often
unaware of any practical political goal Machiavelli might have
intended in his argument.

The publication of *The Prince* generated a complex debate over
its theoretical and moral implications that passed far beyond a
discussion of its immediate practical purpose and its connection
to the political fortunes and aspirations of the Medici family.
Moralists, particularly in England and France, assailed the book
as a compendium of cynical maxims fit only for evil tyrants.
Elizabethan writers were scandalized and intrigued by what they
saw as a typically Machiavellian character—although the character was most often a Senecan villain in doublet and hose. Their
moral indignation was sometimes feigned, but the Elizabethans'
nearly four hundred references to the Florentine Secretary intro-
duced the derogatory terms 'Machiavellian' and 'Machiavellian-
ism' into the English language. Some churchmen branded the
book the work of the devil and its author an atheist, and Machiavelli's first name came to be associated with an already popular
term for the devil: Old Nick. The book enjoyed the dubious
distinction of being attacked from all sides. It was placed on the
Index by the Catholic Church in 1559. Among Protestant

reformers, it symbolized all that was despised in the Italianate culture of High Renaissance Europe: popery, the Roman Curia, 'Reason of State', the Society of Jesus (in anti-Catholic propaganda Machiavelli was linked to Ignatius Loyola), and the moral corruption that Europeans liked to localize within the Italian peninsula but usually experienced closer to home.

As a result of this *succès de scandale*, *The Prince* became known at least indirectly to every sixteenth- and seventeenth-century reader. The traditional view of the 'Machiavellian' Machiavelli finds its best expression in the dramatic literature of the period: Machiavelli appears as a character in the prologue of Marlowe's *The Jew of Malta* (1589), the embodiment of Machiavellian amorality, who remarks: 'I count religion but a childish toy, | And hold there is no sin but ignorance.' More subtle Machiavellian figures include Shakespeare's Richard III and Iago.

In the seventeenth century Machiavelli's original views on republican government began to be studied as assiduously as his interpretation of princely rule. James Harrington, Francis Bacon, and a host of thinkers began to acknowledge Machiavelli's contributions to republican theory and to political realism in the *Discourses on Livy*, *The Art of War*, and *The Florentine Histories*, and they questioned the traditional view of Machiavelli as a teacher of evil. During the Enlightenment, Frederick II of Prussia, at Voltaire's instigation, assailed Machiavelli's immorality, but other thinkers, including Hume, Rousseau, Montesquieu, and Alfieri, hailed the Florentine as the first modern thinker to have exposed the nature of political tyranny. Still later, during the Italian Risorgimento, the period that led to the nineteenth-century unification of Italy, Italians saw the final chapter of *The Prince* as a harbinger of their new nation.

In our own century the book has inspired a number of divergent and sometimes original interpretations. It has been variously read as the first work to analyse the role of the political elite; as the book which established the independence of politics from theology; as an early formulation of the political 'myth' required to galvanize apolitical masses into revolutionary action; as a practical handbook containing timeless rules for the

diplomat; as a useful guide to management and business practices; and, of course, as the handbook of evil. These changing
interpretations in our own era, as well as in the more distant past,
probably reveal as much about the book's readers as they do about
the author's intentions and ideas.

Who Was Niccolò Machiavelli?

Niccolò Machiavelli was born in Florence on 3 May 1469, the
son of Bernardo and Bartolomea de' Nerli, from the neighbour-
hood of Santa Trínita. The Machiavelli had been a prominent
Florentine family. Niccolò's father, however, was neither wealthy
nor powerful. His law degree, and his properties on the outskirts
of Florence, were barely sufficient to guarantee his family a
modest lifestyle. In a letter to Francesco Vettori of 18 March
1513, Niccolò gives us a vivid summary of his youth: 'I was born
in poverty, and at an early age learned how to script rather than
to thrive.'[1]

Poverty did not prevent Bernardo from providing Niccolò with
a good education that enabled him to learn grammar, rhetoric,
and Latin. He never learned Greek, even if Florence was at
the time one of the centres of Greek scholarship in Europe. He
also never learned banking and trade, the two arts in which
Florentines excelled. Unlike the most prominent humanists of
his time, Niccolò was unable to read the great works of Greek
philosophy and historiography in the original. The Latin world
was, on the contrary, perfectly accessible to him. One of the
few facts we know of Machiavelli's youth is that he copied out
Lucretius' *De rerum natura* (*On the Nature of Things*), the great
poem describing the origins of nature—the sea, plants, and
animals—and the condition of man.

From Lucretius, Machiavelli derived his disconsolate and
realistic view of man's condition. Far from being the master of

---

[1] Niccolò Machiavelli, *Machiavelli and His Friends: Their Personal Correspondence*,
ed. and trans. by James B. Atkinson and David Sices (DeKalb: Northern Illinois
University Press, 1996), 222. All citations from Machiavelli's private letters are taken
from this translation unless otherwise indicated.

the universe, man is in fact the victim of nature and of fortune. Man is born naked and bawling. Alone among the animals, he is capable of astonishing cruelty against his fellow human beings. Yet no other creature has such an enormous desire to live and such a thirst for—and need of—the eternal and the infinite.

With this conception of human nature and life, Niccolò Machiavelli appeared on the scene of Florentine politics in 1497. At the time, the major political and moral figure was the Dominican friar Girolamo Savonarola. Through his powerful oratory and his prophetic style, Savonarola had for years been denouncing the corruption of the papacy and the moral decline of Florence. As a remedy against moral corruption that was threatening to produce the irreparable fall of the city in the hands of a tyrannical regime, Savonarola urged the people of Florence to set up a republican government based upon a *Consiglio Maggiore* that was, by sixteenth-century standards, a very large legislative body. The Republic of Florence was actually instituted in December 1494, after the expulsion of the Medici, the family that, with its money and policy of patronage, had been the de facto ruler of Florence since the fifteenth century.

On 15 June 1498, a few weeks after Savonarola had been executed on a charge of heresy, Machiavelli was appointed by the new republican regime *Segretario* (Secretary) of the Second Chancery of the Republic and Secretary of the Ten of Liberty and Peace, a committee in charge of governing military matters and foreign affairs. Machiavelli's main task was to give the governors of Florence the information they needed to enable them to make appropriate and timely decisions. Whereas the political leaders of the Republic held their office for just a few months, Machiavelli's position was in principle a permanent job, with the obvious consequence that a capable and dedicated expert, such as he was, played an important role in the political life of the Republic.

In his position Machiavelli could count on the help of a number of subordinate assistants, such as Agostino Vespucci, Andrea di Romolo, and Biagio Buonaccorsi, who was to become a loyal friend. Unlike his assistants, however, Machiavelli was often called to accompany Florentine ambassadors on delicate diplomatic missions. Even though the missions themselves were neither easy nor rewarding, he loved the opportunity they offered for travelling abroad, gaining direct experience of the mores of different peoples, and of studying their political institutions.

Between 1499 and 1512 Machiavelli had the opportunity to meet the most important political leaders of his time: the King of France, Louis XII; the Emperor Maximilian I; Pope Julius II; and Duke Valentino (Cesare Borgia). He visited several Italian courts, as well as France and the Tyrol. From his missions he was able to gain new insights into real political life and to know directly the minds, the ambitions, the vices, and the (few) virtues of the political leaders who were shaping the destiny of Italy and Europe.

In his diplomatic negotiations, Machiavelli very soon became aware of the political and military weakness of Italy vis-à-vis European nation-states like Spain and France. Divided into five major states (the Duchy of Milan, the Republic of Venice, the Papal State, the Republic of Florence, and the Kingdom of Naples) and a number of independent or semi-independent cities such as Genoa, Lucca, Bologna, Ferrara, and Siena, Italy lacked both political power and military might sufficient to protect the integrity of its territory. All Italian states, including the Republic of Florence, moreover, were relying for their safety on mercenary troops or on the protection of France or Spain.

To rectify this weakness, Machiavelli tried to persuade the political leaders of the Florentine Republic, and above all its highest authority, the Gonfaloniere (Standard-bearer) Pier Soderini, to institute an army, composed first of subjects of the dominion, and later also of Florentine citizens. One of his most important political writings of the period in which he served as Secretary, the *Parole da dirle sopra la provisione del danaio, facto un poco di proemio et di scusa* (*Words to be Spoken on the Law for Appropriating Money, After Giving a Little Introduction and Excuse*), is a powerful oration designed to convince the Florentine leadership that without a good army the Republic's liberty was utterly insecure.[2] Machiavelli succeeded in his project: on 15 February 1506 four hundred soldiers of the newly instituted militia paraded in good order through the streets of Florence. It was his greatest political success.

Neither the new militia nor mercenary troops, and even less the king of France, Florence's alleged protector, were capable of defending the Republic from the assault of Spanish and papal troops in late August 1512. The assault had been carefully prepared by Pope Julius II and the Medici in exile. On 30 August the Spanish troops conquered and sacked Prato, a small town a few miles north of Florence. It was the end of the republican government led by Pier Soderini, and a new government totally controlled by the Medici was promptly set up in its place.

The fall of the Republic was the end of Machiavelli's career as Secretary. On 7 November 1513 he received a letter that relieved him of all his positions. A few days later another letter enjoined him to remain within the dominions of Florence for a year and to pay a surety of one thousand florins. Yet another letter on 17 November forbade him to enter the Palazzo Vecchio, the palace of the government, for a year. Between the end of November and 10 December officers of the new regime subjected him to close investigation to uncover any evidence of malfeasance. They found no such evidence. Even if vast amounts of money had flowed through his hands, Niccolò had served the Republic with complete and impeccable honesty.

Nonetheless, his tribulations were not over. A very poorly planned conspiracy against the Medici was unveiled. Machiavelli was suspected of involvement in it. He was imprisoned and tortured to obtain a confession that would have meant capital punishment. He was able to resist torture, however, and was released from prison on 11 or 12 March 1514, as a result of an amnesty that the Medicean government proclaimed to celebrate the elevation of Cardinal Giovanni de' Medici to the seat of Saint Peter, under the name of Leo X.

---

[2] For an English translation, see *Machiavelli: The Chief Works and Others*, ed. and trans. Allan Gilbert (Durham, NC: Duke University Press, 1989), iii. 1439–43.

Why Machiavelli Wrote The Prince

When Machiavelli sat down in his farmhouse in Sant'Andrea in Percussina, a few miles south of Florence, to write *The Prince*, he was for everyone, and for himself, the 'former Secretary' of the bygone Republic, as he sadly signed a letter of April 1513. However, he did not compose his little treatise in order to please the Medici in the hope of obtaining some kind of political employment within the new regime they had established in Florence in 1512, or in Rome under the protection of the Medici Pope Leo X.

The truth is that Machiavelli did try to obtain a position from the Medici, but he did not write *The Prince* in order to win their favour.[3] He was hoping to be offered a new post in recognition of his unquestionable competence in the 'art of the state' and as a reward for his abilities and impeccable honesty, not as a gift in reward for flattery. As he wrote in the famous letter to Francesco Vettori of 10 December 1513:

Besides, there is my desire that these Medici princes should begin to engage my services, even if they should start out by having me roll along a stone. For then, if I could not win them over, I should have only myself to blame. And through this study of mine [*The Prince*] were it to be read, it would be evident that for the fifteen years while I have been studying the art of the state [*arte dello stato*], I have neither slept nor fooled around, and anybody ought to be happy to utilize someone who has had so much experience at the expense of others. There should be no doubt about my word; for, since I have always kept it, I should not start learning how to break it now. Whoever has been honest and faithful for forty-three years, as I have, is unable to change his nature; my poverty is a witness to my loyalty and honesty.[4]

Had Machiavelli intended to write a work primarily to obtain a job, he would have written a completely different text, full of praise of the Medici and their glorious history, replete with the

---

[3] The reader of *The Prince* should bear in mind that the original title Machiavelli gave to his work was in Latin—*De Principatibus*—and its literal translation in English would read *Of Principalities*. Machiavelli mentions this title in a letter addressed to Francesco Vettori, 10 Dec. 1513. See *Machiavelli and His Friends*, 264.

[4] Ibid.

kind of advice that men like Lorenzo or Leo X liked to hear. Machiavelli knew better than anyone else that the most important rule of successful flattery is to say what pleases the person from whom one expects to obtain favours. In *The Prince* he does exactly the opposite. Instead of repeating the well-established principles that had allowed the Medici to gain control over the city, Machiavelli gave them advice that they were not in the least able to appreciate, and which must surely have irritated them if they had decided to read Machiavelli's work. *The Prince* is a critique of the prevailing Medicean understanding of the art of the state, a policy founded upon a system of favours and patronage designed to ensure substantial control over the republic's institutions.

In *The Prince*, Machiavelli addresses all the key issues concerning the security of a regime like that of the Medici, beginning with the hotly debated theme of the difficulty posed by the large number of supporters of the bygone Republic. With typical briskness, he assures his readers that, unlike what other advisers believed, the truth of the matter is that 'men are much more taken by present concerns than by those of the past, and when they discover benefit in present things, they enjoy it and seek no more. In fact, they will seize every measure to defend the new prince so long as he is not lacking in his duties' (Ch. XXIV).[5]

Machiavelli also rejects the idea that the new regime has to worry about those who were content with the old Republic and sustained it, claiming instead that the true danger comes from the aristocrats who were dissatisfied with it. It will be very difficult for the new prince to turn them into loyal friends, even if they have helped him to attain power (Ch. XX). A new prince must always regard the aristocrats as a serious threat to the state, because they have the means and the audacity to attack him openly if they are dissatisfied. He must therefore distinguish among the nobles between those who are prepared to associate their fate with his and those who are not:

---

[5] All quotations from *The Prince* are taken from the present translation and will be indicated by chapter number in the text proper.

Those who do not commit themselves can be evaluated in two ways. If they act in this manner out of pusillanimity and a natural lack of courage, you should make use of them, especially those who are wise advisers, since in prosperous times they will gain you honour and in adverse times you need not fear them. But when, cunningly and influenced by ambition, they refrain from committing themselves to you, this is a sign that they think more of themselves than of you. The prince should be on his guard against them and fear them as if they were declared enemies, because they will always help to bring about his downfall in adverse times. (Ch. IX)

The Medici, who always presented their regime as a 'civil principality' based upon 'the favour of the common people or with that of the nobility', would hardly have failed to read these lines as strong advice not to seek to ground their power on the nobles' support, as their counsellors were urging them to do (Ch. IX).[6] Against the trite proverb that 'he who builds upon the people builds upon mud' ('chi fonda sul populo fonda sul fango'), endorsed by influential Florentine experts on matters of state, Machiavelli remarks that to secure a civil principality a prince 'must have the friendship of the common people' (Ch. IX). As he explains:

A prince can never make himself secure when the people are his enemy, because there are so many of them; he can make himself secure against the nobles, because they are so few. The worst that a prince can expect from a hostile people is to be abandoned by them, but with a hostile nobility, not only does he have to fear being abandoned but also that they will oppose him. Since the nobles are more perceptive and cunning, they always have time to save themselves, seeking the favours of the side they believe will prevail. Furthermore, a prince must always live with the same common people, but he can easily do without the same nobles, having the power every day to make and unmake them or to take away and restore their power as he sees fit. (Ch. IX)

Subversive though it was, such advice was less scandalous than his comments on the time-honoured Medicean practice of ruling

---

[6] See Maurizio Viroli, *From Politics to Reason of State* (Cambridge: Cambridge University Press, 1992), Ch. 2, for a discussion of this point.

behind the scenes through loyal friends suitably appointed to the important posts of the republic. Civil principalities, Machiavelli warns, collapse as soon as the prince needs to take absolute authority. Since such a need may well arise, it is utterly unwise to believe that a principality in which the prince rules indirectly could last for long. A prince who governs 'by means of public magistrates', Machiavelli explains, is in a highly unstable position because he

depend[s] entirely upon the will of those citizens who are appointed as magistrates. These men can very easily (especially in adverse times) seize the state either by abandoning him or by opposing him. And in such times of danger, the prince has no time for seizing absolute authority, since the citizens and subjects who are used to receiving their orders from the magistrates are not willing to obey his orders in these crises. And in doubtful times he will always find a scarcity of men in whom he can trust. (Ch. IX)

It is difficult to imagine a more eloquent way of saying that the old traditional practice of ruling behind the scenes had to be abandoned, and new ways of governing be put into effect, if a solid state were to be constructed.

Along with the tradition of 'civil government', Machiavelli also attacks the other foundation of the Medicean art of the state, namely the policy of patronage and favours: 'for friendships acquired by a price and not by greatness and nobility of spirit are bought but are not owned, and at the proper time cannot be spent' (Ch. XVII). Favours and honours, he explains, generate at best a loyalty based on gratitude. But since men easily break the bonds of gratitude when they see that it is in their interest to do so, friendships acquired through private favours cannot offer a solid basis for the state. Much more effective than gratitude is fear, sustained by the threat of punishment. If one really regards interest and fear as the most powerful motives for men's conduct, one must conclude that for a prince it is not at all safe to rely on the gratitude of the partisans he has benefited, and that he should rather look for ways of making himself constantly feared. The policy of patronage cannot tie the partisans to the prince as strongly as the security of the state requires.

Once he has dismantled the basic tenets of Florentine wisdom on matters of state, Machiavelli explains that the true art of securing a principality cannot be the skill of controlling public institutions through one's friends, nor does it consist of dissimulating power under the guise of civility. It must first of all be the ability to create and to discipline a militia:

A prince, therefore, must not have any other object nor any other thought, nor must he adopt anything as his art but war, its institutions, and its discipline; because that is the only art befitting one who commands. This discipline is of such efficacy that not only does it maintain those who were born princes, but it enables men of private station on many occasions to rise to that position. On the other hand, it is evident that when princes have given more thought to delicate refinements than to military concerns, they have lost their state. The most important reason why you lose it is by neglecting this art, while the way to acquire it is to be well versed in this art. (Ch. XIV)

By saying that the prince should apply himself to the art of war and work to institute an army composed of his own subjects, Machiavelli was rejecting the Medicean view that the best way to secure a state was to disarm the people:

Now, there has never been a time when a new prince disarmed his subjects. On the contrary, when he has found them unarmed, he has always armed them, because when armed those arms become yours: those whom you suspect become loyal, and those who were loyal remain so, and they become your partisans rather than your subjects. Since all of your subjects cannot be armed, when those you arm receive benefits, you can deal more securely with the others. The difference in treatment toward themselves that they recognize makes them obligated to you. The others excuse you, judging it necessary that those who are in more danger and who hold more responsibility should have a greater reward. (Ch. XX)

For Machiavelli, the old way of building and preserving a regime, theorized over and practised in Florence since the times of Cosimo de' Medici (1389–1464), had to be abandoned in order to embrace a new conception of the art of the state based on the principle that no state is a true dominion unless it is sustained by an army composed of citizens or subjects. For Machiavelli, a state based only on patronage is utterly inadequate to permit a new prince to accomplish great things.[7] He wanted to instruct and motivate a prince who would be capable of liberating Italy from the 'barbarians', as we shall see, not simply of ruling Florence by conferring benefits on this or that individual, giving marriage dowries to the daughters of his partisans, protecting his friends from the magistrates, or other similar acts of patronage.

If his main aim was not to obtain the favour of the Medici, why then did Machiavelli compose *The Prince* in the way he did? Machiavelli composed his treatise in order to prove to everyone, and to himself as well, that although he had been dismissed as Secretary, he knew the art of the state better than anybody else in his time, and better even than the most revered political thinkers of antiquity, in particular Cicero and his modern followers. For this to happen, he had to compose a great work on the art of the state, that is, a work capable of teaching the goals and the means of political action in its greatest sense: the political action of founders and redeemers who have the ability to create new political and legal orders, to unite and emancipate Italy, and, for this reason, to attain perennial glory. Machiavelli's new prince ought to be a new Cyrus, a new Theseus, a new Moses—certainly not a new Cosimo de' Medici. Neither ancient nor modern political thinkers had composed a book designed to teach a founder and a redeemer. Machiavelli composed *The Prince* to provide this missing book, hoping in the process to contribute to the foundation of a new political order and to the emancipation of Italy.[8]

---

[7] See Ch. XVIII and Ch. XXVI ('An exhortation to seize Italy and to free her from the barbarians') for examples of such 'great things' the new prince might accomplish.

[8] In the *Discursus florentinarum rerum post mortem iunioris Laurentii Medices* (*A Discourse on Remodeling the Government of Florence*), composed between November 1520 and February 1521, Machiavelli writes a revealing eulogy of great philosophers such as Aristotle and Plato who were unable to found a republic in reality and had therefore to do so only in writing. For an English translation, see Gilbert (ed.), *Machiavelli: The Chief Works and Others*, i. 101–25.

The Prince *and the* Discourses on Livy

At this juncture the reader might well ask why a republican like Machiavelli should have composed a book to instruct a new prince. Over the centuries scholars have offered two answers. The first is the well-known argument that Rousseau made popular in his *Social Contract*: 'While appearing to instruct kings he has done much to educate the people. Machiavelli's *Prince* is the book of Republicans.'[9] The restoration of Machiavelli's reputation as a republican thinker first began, however, in the late sixteenth century with Alberico Gentili, a jurist educated at Perugia who fled to England and was appointed in 1587 Regius Professor of Civil Law at Oxford. In his *De Legationibus* (*On Embassies*), issued in 1585, he wrote an eloquent eulogy of Machiavelli, whom he praises as the author of the golden (*aureas*) observations on Livy, and as a man of unique prudence and learning. Those who have written against him, Gentili claims, have not understood Machiavelli's ideas at all, and have indeed slandered him. The truth is, Gentili argued, that Machiavelli was

a strong supporter and enthusiast for democracy. [He] was born, educated, and received public honours in a republic. He was extremely hostile to tyranny. Therefore he did not help the tyrant; his intention was not to instruct the tyrant, but by making all his secrets clear and openly displaying the degree of wretchedness to the people . . . while appearing to instruct the prince he was actually educating the people. (*De Legationibus*, 3.9; author's trans.)

Almost a century later, Spinoza resumed the interpretation of Machiavelli as a champion of liberty in his *Tractatus Theologico-Politicus*, published anonymously in 1670. The opinions of that

---

[9] *Le Contrat social* (3. 6). In the 1782 edition the following note was inserted: 'Machiavelli was a decent man and a good citizen. But, being attached to the court of the Medicis, he could not help veiling his love of liberty in the midst of his country's oppression. The choice of his detestable hero, Cesare Borgia, clearly enough shows his hidden aim; and the contradiction between the teaching of *The Prince* and that of the *Discourses on Livy* and the *Florentine Histories* shows that this profound political thinker has so far been studied only by superficial or corrupt readers. The Court of Rome sternly prohibited his book. I can believe it; for it is that court it most clearly portrays' (author's translation).

'wise man', wrote Spinoza, 'seem to me particularly attractive in
view of the well-known fact that he was an advocate of freedom
[*pro libertate fuisse constat*], and also gave some very sound advice
for preserving it'.[10] After Spinoza, the idea of Machiavelli as a
misunderstood republican was authoritatively endorsed in Pierre
Bayle's *Dictionnaire*,[11] and by Diderot in the *Encyclopédie* ('it was
the fault of his contemporaries if they misunderstood what he
was getting at: they took a satire for a eulogy').[12]

For this interpretation to be acceptable we would have to find
in Machiavelli's works or letters compelling evidence that his
claims in *The Prince* are exaggerated in order to instil in the
people feelings of hatred for princes. No such evidence exists,
while abundant textual evidence confirms, on the contrary, that in
The Prince Machiavelli was perfectly serious. In the *Discourses on
Livy*, his republican masterpiece composed between 1513 and
1519, he was to instruct future republican leaders with the same
kind of political advice found in *The Prince*.

The second possible answer to the question of why the republican citizen Machiavelli could also be the author of *The Prince* (to
borrow the title of a seminal essay by Hans Baron), is that after
the fall of the Republic Machiavelli came to the conclusion that
the times called for the institution of a princely government and
therefore set down to write the intellectual foundation of that new
regime, his *Discourses on Livy*.[13] The most compelling textual
evidence for this interpretation is a well-known passage from that
work (*Discourses on Livy*, 1. 18) in which he sums up his discussion of whether it is possible to set up a republican government in
a corrupt city: 'Even if one had to be established or maintained
there, it would be necessary to lead it more towards a monarchical

[10] Benedict De Spinoza, *The Political Works*, ed. A. G. Wernham (Oxford: Clarendon Press, 1958), 313.

[11] Pierre Bayle, *Dictionnaire historique et critique*, 2nd edn, 3 vols. (Rotterdam: Reiner Leers, 1702), article 'Machiavelli', note 'o'.

[12] *Encyclopédie*, article 'Machiavelisme'; I am quoting from the 1765 Neuchatel edition (ix. 793; author's translation).

[13] See Hans Baron, 'Machiavelli the Republican Citizen and the Author of *The Prince*', in *In Search of Florentine Civic Humanism*, 2 vols. (Princeton: Princeton University Press, 1988). The essay was first published in 1961.

than towards a popular government, so that those insolent men
who cannot be improved [by the laws] would be held in check by
an authority which is almost kingly (*podestà quasi regia*).[14] To
understand this passage properly, we must take into consideration
that, for Machiavelli, a good republican government must be a
mixed government which encompasses the principles of the three
classical forms of good political constitutions: monarchy, aris-
tocracy, and popular government. Hence the passage quoted
above means that in times of widespread political corruption and
political and military crisis, a republican government must give a
predominant role to its monarchical element, represented in
Florence by the Gonfaloniere or Standard-bearer, the principal
executive officer of the Republic.

Machiavelli was perfectly capable of putting in writing, as we
shall see, the most subversive political claims. Had he intended to
say that in a corrupt city the only form of government possible
was a principality, he would have openly said it. He never made
such a claim. In the *Discourses on Livy*, on the contrary, he wrote
the most unequivocal defence of the superiority of republican
governments over principalities. In 1520, when Cardinal Giulio
de' Medici consulted him about a possible constitutional reform,
Machiavelli recommended the restoration of a republican government.[15] The simple truth is that Machiavelli did not compose
The Prince to sustain a political transition from a republic to
a principality, but to instruct a founder of a new military and
political order and a redeemer of Italy, as I have already indicated.
Even if Machiavelli, in *The Prince* and elsewhere, indicates that
the people can be the prince, he believes that the work of foundation and redemption can be carried out by one man alone.[16]

---

[14] *Discourses on Livy*, eds. and trans. Julia Conaway Bondanella and Peter Bondanella
(Oxford: Oxford University Press, 2003), 70 (the original Italian phrase at the end of the
citation is inserted by the author). All additional English citations from this work come
from this edition and will be noted in the text proper.

[15] For Machiavelli's recommendations, see the previously mentioned *Discourse on
Remodeling the Government of Florence*, in Gilbert (ed.), *Machiavelli: The Chief Works
and Others*, i. 101–25.

[16] See *Discourses on Livy* (1. 9), where Machiavelli declares that 'in organizing
a republic it is necessary to be alone'. Machiavelli also speaks of the people as a prince
in *The Prince* (Ch. XII); and in line 63 of the poem entitled 'Dell'Ingratitudine'

To these observations we must add another remark, namely that Machiavelli was not a philosopher committed to producing a political system, but an orator engaged in the practice of deliberative rhetoric. For a philosopher, writing one text advocating the principality and another advocating a republican form of government represents a contradiction and a problem; for an orator, such apparent contradictions are less problematic. To state that Machiavelli composed *The Prince* in the manner of an orator means to put forth an interpretation that challenges the view of *The Prince* as a scientific text, indeed the founding work (or one of them) of the modern science of politics.[17]

The Prince *as a Political Oration*

Machiavelli grew up in a city that considered eloquence as the highest ornament of a free political life and a necessary component of the education of a good citizen.[18] To enable young Florentines to learn and effectively practise the art of eloquence, the Republic of Florence and its leading citizens devoted considerable resources in attracting prominent scholars to teach rhetoric at the Studio Fiorentino, the urban institution that eventually became the University of Florence. The words with which Angelo Poliziano, one of the most distinguished humanists of his times, opened his course on rhetoric in 1480 give us a sense of the subject's prestige in Machiavelli's Florence. Nothing is more beautiful, Poliziano explains, than to distinguish oneself in the very art that makes men excel over other animals; nothing is more

('Tercets on Ingratitude or Envy')—an English translation is included in Gilbert (ed.), *Machiavelli: The Chief Works and Others*, ii. 740–4.

[17] The interpretation of Machiavelli as founder of the science of politics is best expressed in Ernst Cassirer, *The Myth of the State* (New Haven, Conn.: Yale University Press, 1946), 130; and in Luigi Russo, *Machiavelli* (Bari: Laterza, 1949), 71.

[18] For discussions of rhetoric, ortatory, and eloquence in Renaissance Florence, see Emilio Santini, *Firenze e i suoi oratori nel Quattrocento* (Milan–Palermo–Naples: Sandron, 1922), 67; Jerrold E. Seigel, *Rhetoric and Philosophy in Renaissance Humanism* (Princeton: Princeton University Press, 1968); and Nancy S. Struever, *The Language of History in the Renaissance* (Princeton: Princeton University Press, 1970).

marvellous than to be able to penetrate the mind and the soul of a multitude, to captivate the people's attention, to drive their will and dominate their passions. Eloquence permits us to embellish and celebrate virtuous men and their actions, and to darken the wicked; to persuade one's dearest fellow citizens to pursue what is useful for the common good and to avoid what is damaging and malignant. Eloquence is like the breastplate and sword with which we defend ourselves and the common good against our enemies and the enemies of the republic. Thanks to eloquent men, Poliziano remarks, states have obtained the greatest advantages, and for this reason oratory has in all times been rewarded and held in the highest honour.[19]

Had Machiavelli not learned the art of rhetoric perfectly well, he would have had no chance of becoming Secretary of the Second Chancery of the Republic of Florence under the supervision of the renowned scholar Marcello Virgilio Adriani.[20] An important, indeed essential, aspect of his assignments was to write letters to inform the leading committees of the Republic (the Signoria and the Ten of Liberty and Peace) on matters of foreign policy and on issues pertaining to the Florentine dominion. Another equally important duty was to compose orations to be delivered before the Great Council of the Republic, or in public ceremonies. Both the letters and the orations required an impeccable mastery of the art of rhetoric.

Machiavelli learned the rules of eloquence by studying the works of the Roman theorists. We know from his father Bernardo's diary (the *Libro di ricordi*) that Niccolò had available in his house the *Rhetorica ad Herennium* (*To Herennius*), wrongly attributed to Cicero, along with Cicero's *De Oratore* (*On the Orator*). Under the rubric of the deliberative genre (the section of rhetoric that teaches how to compose persuasive speeches on political matters), these works offered instructions on how to compose an oration on state affairs. When Machiavelli, between

---

[19] Angelo Poliziano, *Oratio super Fabio Quintiliano et Statii Sylvis*, in Eugenio Garin (ed.), *Prosatori latini del Quattrocento* (Milan–Naples: Ricciardi, n.d.), 883–5.

[20] See Peter Godman, *From Poliziano to Machiavelli: Florentine Humanism in the High Renaissance* (Princeton: Princeton University Press, 1998).

July and December 1513, composed *The Prince*, he followed those instructions from the first to the last page and produced his most splendid oration.[21]

As Roman masters of eloquence prescribed, a good political oration must begin with an appropriate *exordium* that serves the purpose of bringing 'the mind of the auditor into a proper condition to receive the rest of the speech', a task that can be attained by making the auditor or the reader 'well-disposed, attentive, and receptive' (*benivolum, attentum, docilem*) (*De Inv.* 1. 15. 20). Machiavelli diligently puts into practice these rules from the very first page, namely the dedicatory letter entitled 'Nicolaus Macla-vellus magnifico Laurentio Medici iuniori salutem' ('Niccolò Machiavelli to the Magnificent Lorenzo de' Medici'). Machiavelli uses this dedicatory letter as an *exordium* designed to fulfil the important requirement of rendering the reader well-disposed and attentive. In Machiavelli's case, the task was particularly delicate. He had to remove the ill disposition of the Medici and other readers, due not only to the fact that he was the former Secretary of the Republic, but also because he was a man of low social status who dared to write on state matters. Among the various rhetorical strategies outlined by Roman theorists, he chooses to try to gain the reader's benevolence by putting forward the good qualities of his own person, the services he has rendered, his competence on matters of state, the hardships he has endured, and the ill fortune that malignantly strikes him. He writes, in fact, that he has infused the book with his knowledge of the 'deeds of great men' attained through a 'long experience in modern affairs and a continuous study of antiquity', and what he has learned 'in so many years', and with 'so many hardships and dangers' (Dedicatory Letter). To remove the diffidence due to his status, Machiavelli claims that to be of lowly birth actually puts him in the best position to treat matters of state:

Neither do I wish that it be thought presumptuous if a man of low and inferior social condition dares to examine and lay down rules for the

---

[21] For these instructions, see *De Inventione* (*On Invention*), ed. H. M. Hubbel (Cambridge, Mass.: Harvard University Press, 1960), 1. 5. 7.

governance of princes. For just as those who paint landscapes place themselves in a low position on the plain in order to consider the nature of the mountains and the heights, and place themselves high on top of mountains in order to study the plains, in like manner, to know the nature of the people well one must be a prince, and to know the nature of princes well one must be of the people.

After the *exordium*, a proper oration must have a partition in which the orator indicates the subject-matter of his speech. Once again Machiavelli follows the rule of the *ars rhetorica*. He makes it clear that 'I shall set aside any discussion of republics, because I have treated them elsewhere at length. I shall consider solely the principality, weaving together the threads mentioned above as I go, and I shall discuss how these principalities can be governed and maintained' (Ch. II). As he proceeds toward the end of the work, after he has laid down his advice, he diligently completes a summary of the main point of his oration and reminds the reader that he has fulfilled what he had promised, namely, to show how a principality, and particularly a new principality, can be maintained and secured: 'If followed prudently, the things written above make a new prince seem old in power and render him immediately more secure and more established in his state than if he had possessed it for some time' (Ch. XXIV).

The most compelling evidence for the rhetorical nature of *The Prince* is Chapter XXVI, entitled 'An exhortation to seize Italy and to free her from the barbarians', which brings the treatise to a dramatic conclusion. Without it, Machiavelli's essay would have been incomplete because it would have lacked the device which is most necessary in order to arouse the readers' emotions and move them to do what he was urging them to accomplish. Following the rules of the *ars rhetorica*, Machiavelli constructs the 'Exhortation' to arouse indignation and compassion; the former by stressing the cruelties and insolences that the barbarians have inflicted upon Italy ('crudeltà et insolenzie barbare'), the latter by pointing to Italy's weakness and helplessness: 'more enslaved than the Hebrews, more servile than the Persians, more scattered than the Athenians: without a leader, without order, beaten, despoiled, ripped apart, overrun, and having suffered every sort of ruin' (Ch. XXVI). Far from being inconsistent with the rest of the work, the 'Exhortation' is the perfect ending.

Roman authorities recommended that a very effective way to persuade and move a person or a council to adopt a particular policy is to offer examples taken from history. Exemplification, as the author of the *Ad Herennium* wrote, 'renders a thought more brilliant when used for no other purpose than beauty; clearer, when throwing more light upon what was somewhat obscure; more plausible, when giving the thought a greater verisimilitude; more vivid, when expressing everything so lucidly that the matter can, I may almost say, be touched by the hand'.[22] Of various types of examples, those taken from recent and ancient history are particularly effective for persuading the audience to accept the view the orator is putting forth. As the reader will notice, Machiavelli masterfully resorts to ancient and modern historical examples to make his arguments vivid, lucid, and persuasive, as well as to instil the desire to imitate the great political and military leaders: 'no one should marvel if, in speaking of principalities that are completely new as to their ruler and form of government, I cite the greatest of examples', because a prudent man ('uno uomo prudente') must always follow the footsteps of great men, and even if 'one's own virtue does not match theirs, at least it will have the smell of it' (Ch. VI).

Another fundamental rule of eloquence was that one of the most effective ways to explain and teach a concept is to place it before the eyes of the reader or the listeners by using similes, images, and metaphors. Machiavelli is also a master of this technique. When he explains, against Cicero's doctrine, that a prince must be capable of using force and fraud, he mentions the images of the lion and the fox: 'Since, then, a prince must know how to use well the nature of the beast, he should choose from among the beasts the fox and the lion; for the lion cannot defend itself from traps, while the fox cannot protect itself from the wolves. It is therefore necessary to be a fox, in order to recognize the traps,

---

[22] *Ad Herennium* (*To Herennius*), ed. H. Caplan (Cambridge, Mass.: Harvard University Press, 1954), 4. 49. 62.

and a lion, in order to frighten the wolves' (Ch. XVIII). When he wants the readers to grasp fully his injunction that a prince should never rely upon auxiliary armies, he finds

a figure from the Old Testament that suits this topic. David offered himself to Saul to fight Goliath, the Philistine challenger. In order to give him courage, Saul armed him with his own armour, which David cast off after putting it on, declaring that with it he could not test his true worth. He therefore wished to meet the enemy with his own sling and his own knife. In short, the weapons of others slide off your back, weigh you down, or tie you up. (Ch. XIII)

Latin masters of eloquence had not only laid down the rules that ought to govern the correct subdivision of a political oration and the effective use of ornaments, but had also described the main goal that the orator has to have in view when offering his counsels, and had outlined the specific issues that a speech or treatise on matters of state must discuss. As to the goal, the Latin authorities stressed that counsellors on matters of state have to offer advice that is advantageous (*utile*) and honest (*honestus*). Speeches before deliberative bodies, Cicero explains in the *De Inventione*, are about what is honest (*quid honestus*) and what is advantageous (*quid utile*). Unlike Aristotle, who accepts advantage as the end of deliberative speeches, Cicero remarks that the end is 'both honesty and advantage' (*De Inv.* 2. 4. 12; 2. 51.156). He then specifies that all actions are honourable that fulfil the requirements of virtue, which he defines as 'the habit of mind in harmony with reason and the order of nature'. Advantage in matters of state has two parts: security (*incolumitas*) and power (*potentia*). (*De Inv.* 2. 66. 169). Advantage primarily consists in those things that protect the safety of the state, namely fields, harbours, money, the fleet, sailors, soldiers, and allies, and in those things that pertain to the greatness of the state, such as money, friendships, and alliances (*De Inv.* 2. 55. 168).

The *Ad Herennium* indicates advantage (*utilitas*) as the overarching goal of political advice, and divides advantage into security (*tuta*) and honesty (*honestas*). The text then subdivides

security into might and craft (*vim et dolum*) and honesty into the
right and the praiseworthy (*rectum et laudabile*). Under the head-
ing of might are to be discussed issues pertaining to armies, fleets,
arms, engines of war, and the recruitment of manpower; craft is
exercised by means of 'money, promises, dissimulations, and
deception'. Right consists in virtue and duty. Its subdivisions
are, as for Cicero, wisdom (*prudentia*), justice (*iustitia*), fortitude
(*fortitudo*), and temperance (*temperantia*). The praiseworthy
(*laudabile*) is 'what produces an honourable remembrance, at the
time of the event and afterwards' (*Ad Her.* 3. 4. 7).

Machiavelli arranges the chapters of *The Prince* according to
this order. He discusses first the issues pertaining to the security
of principalities; then he offers his advice concerning the qualities
that make a prince praised and honoured. In more detail, he
addresses the issue of security by discussing the territory, the
number of men the prince can count upon, the strength of his
enemies, and the quality of his army. On these issues he puts
forth his views concerning the specific kind of difficulties that
new princes have to face in the phase of consolidation of their
power, and argues that a new prince is insecure because 'men
gladly change their ruler, thinking to better themselves', and
because 'a new prince must always harm his new subjects, both
with his soldiers as well as with countless other injuries involved
in his new conquest' (Ch. III).

On the issue of the territorial extension of the state, he stresses
that it is much easier to govern territories lying in the same country and whose people speak the same language than over territories belonging to a different country. In the latter case, Machiavelli
suggests that the best thing a new prince can do is to go and live
there, or to establish colonies in a few places. At the same time,
the prince should become the protector of the neighbouring
minor powers, and try to weaken those who are powerful within
the country itself.

Machiavelli brings the discussion on the might of the state to
an end in Chapter X, where he addresses the issue 'How the
strength (*vires*) of all principalities should be measured'. He
explains that the difference between a prince who has sufficient

territory and power to defend himself and one who will always need some help from others consists in the fact that the former can put together an army that is good enough to fight a battle against any power that attacks him, while the latter cannot (Ch. X). As he stresses with typical briskness in Chapter XII, the might that a prince must possess to be secure has to be such that it permits him to defend his state without anybody's help. The real security of the state, Machiavelli warns, therefore requires that the prince can count on an army composed of his own subjects.

Having accomplished the task of instructing his readers on how to secure the might of the state, Machiavelli considers the issues that properly pertain to craft (*dolus*): that is, taxation, promises, dissimulation, and deception. In discussing these issues, Machiavelli directs a number of severe criticisms towards the conventional political wisdom that prescribes how a good prince must be generous and always keep his word. If a prince wants to keep up a reputation for being generous, Machiavelli remarks:

it is necessary for him not to neglect any possible means of sumptuous display; in so doing, such a prince will always use up all his resources in such displays and will be eventually obliged, if he wishes to maintain his reputation for generosity, to burden the people with excessive taxes and to do all those things one does to procure money. This will begin to make him hateful to his subjects and, if he becomes impoverished, he will be held in low regard by everyone. (Ch. XVI)

A prudent prince should therefore be parsimonious. In this way his revenues will always be sufficient to defend his state 'without overburdening his people' (Ch. XVI).

As for promises, dissimulation, and deception, Machiavelli condenses his views in Chapter XVIII and offers here one of his most subversive pieces of advice: 'A wise ruler, therefore, cannot and should not keep his word when such an observance would be to his disadvantage and when the reasons that caused him to make a promise are removed.' And he adds, a few lines later, that to put the above advice effectively into practice, the prince must be a

great feigner and dissembler. He goes so far as to write that
'I shall dare to assert this: that having them and always observing them [the qualities of faith and honesty] is harmful, but
appearing to observe them is useful' (Ch. XVIII).

Honesty and Virtue

The context of the *ars rhetorica* also helps us to understand
properly the central issue of *The Prince*, namely, the main goal
that guides Machiavelli's advice. As we have seen, the good orator
must direct his counsel toward interest (*utilitas*), and indicate
which of the two components of advantage, security or honesty, is
his main concern. If possible the orator should try to prove that
his advice meets all the aspects of security or honesty; if the
matter does not allow it, he should 'in speaking set forth as many
as do'. (*Ad Her.* 3. 4. 8). Machiavelli clearly states that his goal is
to write 'something useful (*utile*) for anyone who understands
it' (Ch. XV). He also indicates that his counsels are directed
to make a new prince both secure and praised. If followed
prudently, Machiavelli writes in Chapter XXIV, the things
written above make a new prince seem long-established in power
and render him immediately more secure (*sicuro*) and more
established in his state than if he had possessed it for some time.
In Chapter XVIII, concluding the discussion on the conflict
between honesty and advantage, he stresses that if the prince
conquers and maintains the state, 'his methods will always be
judged honourable and praised by all'. Which is to say that
Machiavelli wants to persuade the readers of his oration that if
a new prince follows his advice, he will attain both security and
honour—the two components of advantage as described in the
Ad Herennium.

Scholars have stressed that Machiavelli does not at all address
the topics of honesty and right. Machiavelli, writes Quentin
Skinner, not only questions the Ciceronian ideal of harmony
between the *honestum* and the *utile* (the good and the useful), but
also endorses the subversive suggestion that 'the question of what
is *utile* in such matters of statecraft may have no connection with

what is *onesto* at all'.[23] Serious political debate, John Tinkler has written in a seminal essay, 'which is directed at advising future action, must be practical, and must therefore take *utilitas* [advantage] as its ultimate aim. Certainly, this was the aim laid down in both the *Rhetorica ad Herennium* and the *De Inventione*, the two most important classical rhetorical treatises in both the Middle Ages and the Renaissance. It is this ultimate concern of deliberative rhetoric with *utilitas* that sheds light on Machiavelli's concern with political success.'[24]

In fact, Machiavelli urges the prince to pursue 'a righteous cause' when he encourages him to commit himself to the liberation of Italy (Ch. XXVI). However, he worries above all about praise and blame, as the title of Chapter XV explicitly indicates ('Of those things for which men, and particular princes, are praised or blamed'). He wants his work to be understood as a text that teaches the prince to follow the virtues that would bring him security and honour, and, if necessary, abandon those that would surely cause him to lose his state and be condemned to perennial infamy. To explain this point, he resorts to the well-known rhetorical device of redescribing as vices the actions that other theorists on state matters qualify as virtues, but which in fact lead to the loss of the state, then redefines as virtues those actions that are considered to be vices, but which lead to the state's preservation.

As Roman rhetoricians had explained, virtue and vices are neighbours.[25] What counts as a virtue can therefore be redescribed

---

[23] Quentin Skinner, *Reason and Rhetoric in the Philosophy of Hobbes* (Cambridge: Cambridge University Press, 1996), 44.

[24] John F. Tinkler, 'Praise and Advice; Rhetorical Approaches in More's *Utopia* and Machiavelli's *The Prince*', *Sixteenth Century Journal*, 19 (1988), 198. Another passage from Tinkler's essay deserves quotation: 'Many indications suggest that Machiavelli knew precisely what he was doing in rhetorical terms: his plain style and rejection of superficial ornament; his insistence on his personal experience of politics; his rejection of flattery and mere praise; and, above all, his characteristically deliberative concern with advice that is *utile*, all suggest that he was conscious of replacing a demonstrative with a deliberative approach.' While I do not believe that Machiavelli was concerned with replacing the demonstrative or epideictic genre, the genre to be used when we speak to praise a person, with the deliberative approach, I think that this passage illuminates very well the rhetorical nature of *The Prince*.

[25] See Skinner, *Reason and Rhetoric in the Philosophy of Hobbes*, 151–5.

as vice and what counts as a vice can be redescribed as a virtue, if the necessity to achieve the security of the state so requires. Machiavelli writes that a prince should 'know how to escape' the

infamy of those vices that would take the state away from him, and be on guard against those vices that will not take it from him, whenever possible. But if he cannot, he need not concern himself unduly if he ignores these less serious vices. Moreover, he need not worry about incurring the infamy of those vices without which it would be difficult to save the state. Because, carefully taking everything into account, he will discover that something which appears to be a virtue, if pursued, will result in his ruin; while some other thing which seems to be a vice, if pursued, will secure his safety and his well-being. (Ch. XV)

Actions which are usually blamed as wicked can be redescribed as good and recommended. In the discussion of cruelty in Chapter VIII, Machiavelli introduces the distinction between well-committed and badly committed cruelties: to the former kind belong cruelties 'that are carried out in a single stroke, done out of necessity to protect oneself, and then are not continued but are instead converted into the greatest possible benefits for the subjects'; to the latter, cruelties that, 'although few at the outset, increase with the passing of time instead of disappearing'. Machiavelli openly admits that here he is redescribing evil as good, and promptly excuses himself: 'if it is permitted to speak well of evil' (Ch. VIII). A few lines above he had used the same rhetorical device, this time in a contrary fashion, namely, to claim that some kinds of action cannot be *called* virtuous even if they assure the preservation of the princes' power. Of the infamous Agathocles he says: 'Still, it cannot be called virtue to kill one's fellow citizens, to betray allies, to be without faith, without pity, without religion; by these means, one can acquire power but not glory' (Ch. VIII).

Another way to solve the conflict between honesty and security that Roman rhetoricians laid down was the topic of necessity. The greatest necessity, writes Cicero in *De Inventione*, is that of doing what is honourable, next comes the necessity of security, last the necessity—of much lesser weight—of convenience. (*De Inv.* 2. 58. 173). This ordering can be altered, however, if security is really at stake. In this case, the orator can put security before honour. Honour, momentarily lost, can be later recovered by courage and diligence (*De Inv.* 2. 58. 174). An argument based on honesty and fairness is always a strong one, but it can be countered if we prove that the position we are advocating is 'necessary', and in deliberative rhetoric necessity has to be referred to the security of the state (*De Inv.* 1. 51. 96; 2. 58. 74)

Machiavelli grants that the humanists' advice that the prince should never abandon the path of virtue is fair. Nonetheless, he stresses that there are indeed circumstances in which it is necessary to abandon the path of honesty. 'It is necessary', he writes, for a prince to learn 'how not to be good' (Ch. XV). Machiavelli's wording on this matter is extremely precise: a man who wants 'to profess goodness at all times' will inevitably fail because he is surrounded by many unscrupulous men. Hence, 'it is necessary for a prince who wishes to maintain himself to learn how not to be good, and to use this knowledge or not to use it according to necessity' (Ch. XV). A few lines later he restates the same point in even clearer terms: 'And I know that everyone will admit it would be a very praiseworthy thing to find in a prince the qualities mentioned above that are held to be good. But since it is neither possible to have them nor to observe them all completely, because the human condition does not permit it, a prince must be prudent enough to know how to escape the infamy of those vices that would take the state away from him . . .' A prince or a ruler must 'not depart from the good', as long as he can (*potendo*); but he 'should know how to enter into evil forced by necessity (*necessitato*) (Ch. XVIII).

By preserving the state the prince attains honour and praise. His reputation will further increase if his actions display grandeur, courage, seriousness, and strength, and if he endeavours in all his actions 'to achieve the reputation of a great man of outstanding intelligence', as Machiavelli subsequently urges (Ch. XXI). If we add to that the other part of Machiavelli's advice, namely, that the prince should avoid being rapacious and show himself a lover of talent, reward those who excel in any art, encourage the citizens to follow quietly their ordinary occupations, both in trade and agriculture and every other kind, and should display affability and munificence (Ch. XXI), we have a full sense of Machiavelli's advice: honour is securely attained by preserving the state, and by displaying greatness of spirit, justice, generosity, strength; that is, by re-entering the path of virtue. Machiavelli's overall advice to a new prince does, therefore, embrace all the aspects of interests—security, right, honour, and virtue—as the *Ad Herennium* had recommended.

The fact that Machiavelli was following the teaching of the Roman rhetoricians does not at all diminish the intended subversive meaning of *The Prince*. Against the conventional Ciceronian precept that to attain glory and preserve his state the prince must follow the virtues, Machiavelli states, in the clearest possible way, that if a prince always wants to behave according to moral virtues he will surely lose his state and attain no glory at all. Most of the passages of *The Prince* which have gained Machiavelli a sinister reputation are explicit attacks on the main principles of Ciceronian political theory.

Wrong, Cicero remarked in *De Officiis*, may be done 'by force or by fraud'; both are bestial: 'fraud seems to belong to the cunning fox, force to the lion. Both ways are wholly unworthy of man, but fraud is the more contemptible.'[26] Machiavelli's famous response comes in Chapter XVIII:

you must know that there are two modes of fighting: one in accordance with the laws, the other with force. The first is proper to man, the second to beasts. But because the first, in many cases, is not sufficient, it becomes necessary to have recourse to the second: therefore, a prince must know how to make good use of the natures of both the beast and the man. This rule was taught to princes symbolically by the writers of antiquity: they recounted how Achilles and many others of those ancient princes were given to Chiron the centaur to be raised and cared for under his discipline. This can only mean that, having a half-beast and half-man as a teacher, a prince must know how to

---

[26] Cicero, *De Officiis* (*On Duties*), ed. Walter Miller (Cambridge, Mass.: Harvard University Press, 1913), i. 13. 41.

employ the nature of the one and the other; for the one without the other is not lasting.

Commenting upon the foundations of political authority, Cicero had stressed that 'of all the motives, none is better adapted to secure influence and hold it fast than love; nothing is more foreign to that end than fear'. From this principle he had derived a straightforward piece of advice: 'let us, then, embrace this policy, which appeals to every heart and is the strongest support not only of security but also of influence and power—namely, to banish fear and cleave to love. And thus we shall most easily secure success both in private and in public life' (*De Off.* 2. 7. 24). On this issue too, Machiavelli rejects Cicero's views. Men are 'ungrateful, fickle, simulators and deceivers, avoiders of danger, and greedy for gain. While you work for their benefit, they are completely yours, offering you their blood, their property, their lives, and their sons, as I said above, when the need is far away. But when it draws nearer to you, they turn away' (Ch. XVII). It is therefore better to be feared than to be loved, if one cannot be both, because 'men are less hesitant about injuring someone who makes himself loved than one who makes himself feared'.

Cicero had proclaimed that 'no cruelty can be expedient and that cruelty is most abhorrent to human nature, whose lead we ought to follow'. To which Machiavelli responds, in Chapter VIII: 'well used are those cruelties (if it is permitted to speak well of evil) that are carried out in a single stroke, done out of necessity to protect oneself, and then are not continued but are instead converted into the greatest possible benefits for the subjects'. Therefore, as he writes in Chapter XVII, 'every prince must desire to be considered merciful and not cruel; nevertheless, he must take care not to use such mercy badly. Cesare Borgia was considered cruel; none the less, this cruelty of his brought order to the Romagna, united it, and restored it to peace and loyalty.'

Radical as it is, however, Machiavelli's critique of Ciceronian political ethics is intended to restrict the range of its validity, rather than to dismiss it altogether. Ciceronian precepts are to be followed, except in situations of necessity when the security of

the state is at stake. In *Discourses on Livy* (3. 40), Machiavelli calls
the use of fraud 'detestable'; yet 'in waging war it is, nevertheless,
a laudable and glorious thing'. A fraud which involves breaking
your word or the contracts you have made, Machiavelli clarifies, is
not glorious at all: 'this kind of deceit, even though it may on
occasion gain state and kingdom for you, as was discussed above,
will never bring you glory.' What turns a fraud into a praiseworthy and glorious deed is the fact that a prince or a ruler uses it
'with an enemy who does not trust you, and that especially
involves waging war'.[27]

God, the Friend of Founders

The Ciceronian themes and ideas which Machiavelli criticizes were
rather influential in shaping the language of the Florentine political
elite, as we can see from the records of the Pratiche, the advisory
bodies of the Republic of Florence. In the Pratica of 17 July 1512,
for instance, two leading citizens forcefully reiterated that the
Republic must keep its word and honour its commitments in international affairs. A speaker even goes as far as to say that death is
preferable to the violation of one's word.[28] Other citizens, on the
contrary, reiterate the principle that honesty must have priority over
interest unless necessity compels us to put security above any other
consideration.[29] Pier Soderini himself, the Gonfaloniere of Florence

[27] Although Machiavelli surely intended to criticize the Ciceronian ideal of the good
prince, it is less certain that he also intended to revolutionize the genre of Quattrocento
advice-books for princes. Quentin Skinner has made this point in *The Foundations of
Modern Political Thought* (Cambridge: Cambridge University Press, 1978), i. 113–38.
The main reason to doubt this is that such texts were hardly available to him. See also
Skinner's *Machiavelli* (Oxford: Oxford University Press, 1981), 31–47; Allan H.
Gilbert, *Machiavelli's Prince and its Forerunners* (Durham, NC: Duke University Press,
1938); and Felix Gilbert, 'The Humanist Concept of the Prince and *The Prince* of
Machiavelli', *Journal of Modern History*, 11 (1939), 449–83. On 'advice-to-princes'
texts, by Patrizi, Carafa, and Pontano, associated with the Aragon court in Naples, see
Carlo Dionisotti, *Machiavellerie* (Turin: Einaudi, 1980), 113.

[28] See *Consulte e Pratiche 1505–1512*, ed. Denise Fachard (Geneva: Droz, 1988),
320–5.

[29] Ibid. 353. See also Felix Gilbert, 'Florentine Political Assumptions in the Period of
Savonarola and Soderini', *Journal of the Warburg and Courtauld Institutes*, 20 (1957), 195.

from 1502 to 1512, under whom Machiavelli served as Secretary, fell from power and was not able to defend the Republic effectively because his commitment to honesty prevented him from using extraordinary means against the supporters of the Medici.[30] The Florentine political ethos, then, needed to be emended from a too strict observance of Ciceronian principles, if one wanted, as Machiavelli did, to create the intellectual and moral premises for a political leadership capable of founding a new and better political order and of redeeming Italy.

In *The Prince* Machiavelli mounts two distinct lines of intellectual and political attack, one against the baseness of Medicean statecraft, the other against the too-strict Ciceronian conception of politics. Against both traditions, he elaborates a new 'art of the state'. He openly declares himself to be an expert in this art. 'If I could talk with you,' he wrote to Francesco Vettori on 9 April 1513, 'I could not help but fill your head with castles in air, because Fortune has seen to it that since I do not know how to talk about either the silk or the wool trade, or profits or losses, I have to talk about politics' ('mi conviene ragionare dello stato').[31] Vettori, like all those who knew him well, was pleased to acknowledge Machiavelli's expertise: 'I know you have such intelligence that although two years have gone by since you left the shop I do not think you have forgotten the craft' ('non credo abbiate dimenticato l'arte').[32]

The two most glorious aspects of the art of the state are for Machiavelli the foundation of new political orders and the redemption of peoples. The core of *The Prince* is precisely dedicated to these aspects of political action. As a skilled political orator, he makes his most important points at the end of his work. In Chapter XXIV, he promises the founder of 'a new principality', adorned and consolidated with good laws, good arms, good friends, and good examples, that he will obtain 'double glory'. In the last chapter (Ch. XXVI), he assures Italy's future redeemer that the imitation of such legendary figures as Moses, Theseus,

---

[30] See *Discourses on Livy*, 1. 52; 3. 3; 3. 9; and 3. 30.
[31] *Machiavelli and His Friends*, 225.
[32] Ibid. 294 (3 Dec. 1514).

and Cyrus is indeed possible: although these men 'were rare and marvellous, they were nevertheless men'. He also offers these founders and redeemers another important piece of assurance to further motivate them: God's friendship. 'Nor was God more a friend to them than to you.' God will be the friend of a redeemer of Italy because his cause is just; and He will demonstrate His friendship by helping the redeemer to accomplish his extraordinary deed, as He did with Moses: 'we now see here extraordinary, unprecedented signs brought about by God: the sea has opened up; a cloud has shown you the path; the rock has poured water forth; here, manna has rained; everything has converged for your greatness. The rest you must do yourself. God does not wish to do everything, in order not to take our free will from us and part of the glory that is ours' (Ch. XXVI).

God does not want to act on behalf of founders and redeemers, but He is surely prepared to sustain their efforts with His friendship because He loves justice and good political order.[33] He is even prepared to forgive them for the cruelties they are forced to perpetrate in order to attain their goal. Moses himself resorted to cruelty and lies, we read in Exodus 32: 25–8, to lead the Hebrews to the Promised Land;[34] yet God remained his friend.

As scholars over the centuries have stressed, Machiavelli writes that a new prince must be prepared to act 'against religion'. But they have failed to recognize, with few exceptions, that he never writes, in *The Prince* or elsewhere, that a new prince should feel entitled to act against God. For Machiavelli, to act 'against religion' means to act against the Christian religion falsely interpreted, 'according to an ideal of freedom from earthly toil' (*ozio*), and not 'according to one of exceptional ability' (*virtù*), that the Catholic Church has unfortunately spread about Italy (*Discourses*

---

[33] See the previously cited *Discourse on Remodeling the Government of Florence*, in Gilbert (ed.), *Machiavelli: The Chief Works and Others*, i. 101–25. See also *Allocuzione ad un magistrato* (*Allocution Addressed to a Magistrate*), in Alessandro Montevecchi (ed.), *Opere di Niccolò Machiavelli: Istorie fiorentine e altre opere storiche e politiche* (Turin: UTET, 1986), i. 135–9. See also Sebastian De Grazia, *Machiavelli in Hell* (Princeton: Princeton University Press, 1989).

[34] Machiavelli also explicitly refers to Exodus in the *Discourses on Livy* (3: 30).

on Livy, 2. 2). If correctly interpreted, Christian religion would teach men 'to exalt and defend our native land' (*Discourses on Livy*, 2. 2). This was Machiavelli's true religion, as he himself reveals in a dramatic and moving confession he made to Francesco Vettori toward the end of his life in a letter dated 16 April 1527: 'I love my native city more than my own soul.'[35]

Contrary to the black legend of an atheistic or anti-religious Machiavelli, there is nothing in *The Prince* that goes against God or against what Machiavelli believed to be true Christian moral and political teaching. Without taking into account this aspect of Machiavelli's thinking, we cannot hope to grasp the theory of the foundation of states that makes *The Prince* such a unique and original work.

MAURIZIO VIROLI

[35] *Machiavelli and His Friends*, 416.

TRANSLATOR'S NOTE

THE present translation is an entirely new version of Machiavelli's masterpiece based upon the Italian critical edition published in 1994 by Giorgio Inglese—recognized by most Machiavelli scholars as the best text we have available today—and subsequently reprinted by Rinaldo Rinaldi in 1998 with minor changes. Thus, this new Oxford World's Classics edition can fairly claim to have been based upon a more authoritative text than previously published translations.

This new version of *The Prince* aims at accuracy but also at a more pleasing and readable English prose style than is possible if a translation respects Machiavelli's word order too closely. I have often broken up Machiavelli's longer, sometimes convoluted Ciceronian periods into more readable passages in English, rendered by several sentences instead of several dependent clauses. The end result, I believe, is that Machiavelli's ideas shine through more convincingly than they did in previous translations (including the one I did with Mark Musa in 1979 that was subsequently reprinted with revisions in 1984 by Oxford World's Classics). And yet Machiavelli's peerless prose style remains as persuasive in English as it has always been in the original Italian.

This edition also contains entirely new notes, and many more of them than accompanied my earlier version. The historical events Machiavelli cites from Greek and Roman antiquity, as well as those from his own times, are confusing to a reader without any special expertise in classics or in Italian Renaissance history. References to figures from history are explained in a separate Glossary of Proper Names, while the Notes themselves concentrate on critical problems or historical information. I have relied very heavily upon the historical data in Rinaldo Rinaldi's superb edition of Machiavelli's *Prince* and *Discourses on Livy* in two volumes. This translation follows Inglese's critical edition for the indentation of paragraphs, the original chapter titles in Latin, the original quotations Machiavelli cites from Latin works, and any questionable reading of the manuscript tradition itself.

Machiavelli's *Prince* is both a revolutionary work of political theory and a masterpiece of Italian Renaissance prose style. More than most political thinkers, Machiavelli's ideas are shaped by the style in which he expresses them. This explains in some measure why *The Prince* continues to be translated and retranslated, since scholars and editors who may agree on the content of what Machiavelli has written are often not satisfied with the way in which his translators have turned his prose into English. In addition, scholarly views on Machiavelli change, and such interpretations must, of necessity, have an influence upon our translations.

Much of the scholarship of the past three decades has focused upon Machiavelli's political vocabulary. Important terms such as *virtù, stato, occasione, fortuna, prudenza, libertà, ordini, vivere civile, gloria,* and *dominio* often have no single and systematic equivalent in the English language. The translator must rely on sensitivity to the context surrounding the word to determine its precise meaning. *Virtù*, the quintessential quality of the new ruler in *The Prince*, for example, may be translated into English as 'virtue' so long as the reader remembers that Machiavelli's 'virtue' is a masculine, even heroic quality, and that it generally connotes 'ingenuity', 'skill', 'ability', or 'prowess'. On rare but important occasions, however, the word does mean 'virtue' in the sense of certain traditional moral qualities that are opposed to certain traditional vices. *Fortuna* is another problematic term. Machiavelli personifies this force as a woman in one of his most famous passages in *The Prince*; his use of the term refers to the philosophical concept of the forces that work against human order and planning, an idea that classical antiquity frequently embodied as a goddess. However, on occasion *fortuna* in Machiavelli simply means good or bad luck. In this translation, 'Fortune' is capitalized when it refers to the abstract or personified philosophical concept.

I am very grateful to Maurizio Viroli for his generous and extremely helpful suggestions during the preparation of this new English translation.

PETER BONDANELLA

SELECT BIBLIOGRAPHY

Italian Editions

The critical edition upon which the present translation is based, a scholarly work considered to have established the best possible text that we have available today, is Giorgio Inglese's *De principatibus* (Rome: Istituto storico italiano per il Medio Evo, 1994). Inglese's fundamental editorial work has been reprinted by Rinaldo Rinaldi in *Opere di Niccolò Machiavelli: De Principatibus, Discorso sopra la prima Deca di Tito Livio (I–II)*, vol. I, part 1 (Turin: UTET, 1999). The other volumes of this important UTET edition provide the most useful and reliable Italian texts available: Rinaldo Rinaldi (ed.), *Opere di Niccolò Machiavelli: Discorsi sopra la prima deca di Tito Livio (III), Dell'arte della guerra*, Dalle *Legazioni*, vol. I, part 2 (Turin: UTET, 1999); Alessandro Montevecchi (ed.), *Opere di Niccolò Machiavelli: Istorie fiorentine e altre opere storiche e politiche*, vol. II (Turin: UTET, 1986); Franco Gaeta (ed.), *Opere di Niccolò Machiavelli: Lettere*, vol. III (Turin: UTET, 1984); and Luigi Blasucci (ed.), *Opere di Niccolò Machiavelli: Scritti letterari*, vol. IV (Turin: UTET, 1996). Other editions of Machiavelli's complete works may also be consulted: *Tutte le opere storiche e letterarie*, ed. Guido Mazzoni and Mario Casella (Florence: G. Barbera, 1929); Mario Martelli's single-volume edition, *Tutte le opere* (Florence: Sansoni, 1971); or *Il principe e Discorsi sopra la prima deca di Tito Livio*, ed. Giuliano Procacci and Sergio Bertelli (Milan: Feltrinelli, 1960).

Other Italian editions of *The Prince*, in spite of their age, are still useful for their commentary on the text. These include: *Il principe*, ed. L. Arthur Burd (Oxford: Clarendon Press, 1891); *Il principe di Niccolò Machiavelli*, ed. Giuseppe Lisio (Florence: Sansoni, 1899); *Il principe e altri scritti*, ed. Gennaro Sasso (Florence: La Nuova Italia, 1963); *Il principe*, eds. Federico Chabod and Luigi Firpo (Turin: Einaudi, 1966); and *Il principe e altre opere politiche*, ed. Delio Cantimori (Milan: Garzanti, 1976).

English Translations

There are several major anthologies of Machiavelli's works in English. *The Historical, Political, and Diplomatic Works of Niccolò Machiavelli*, trans. Christian E. Detmold, 4 vols. (Boston: James R. Osgood, 1882) is still worth consulting. The most recent attempt to translate most of Machiavelli's major works in a single English edition by a single hand is *Machiavelli: The Chief Works and Others*, ed. and trans. Allan Gilbert, 3 vols. (Durham, NC: Duke University Press, 1965). For a paperback edition of major selections from Machiavelli's political, historical, and literary works (including private letters), see *The Portable Machiavelli* (New York: Penguin, 1979), ed. and trans. Peter Bondanella and Mark Musa.

Individual translations of *The Prince* are numerous, and differ widely in quality; none of those currently available are based upon the fundamental Inglese critical edition. The most useful are the following: *The Prince*, ed. and trans. George Bull (New York: Penguin, 1961); *The Prince*, ed. and trans. James B. Atkinson (Indianapolis: Bobbs-Merrill, 1976); *The Prince: A Norton Critical Edition*, ed. and trans. Robert M. Adams (New York: Norton, 1977); *The Prince*, ed. Peter Bondanella and trans. Peter Bondanella and Mark Musa (Oxford: Oxford University Press, 1984); *The Prince*, ed. and trans. Harvey C. Mansfield, Jr. (Chicago: University of Chicago Press, 1985); *The Prince*, ed. and trans. Quentin Skinner and Russell Price (Cambridge: Cambridge University Press, 1988); *The Prince*, ed. and trans. David Wootton (Indianapolis: Hackett, 1995); *The Prince*, ed. and trans. Angelo M. Codevilla (New Haven, Conn.: Yale University Press, 1997); and *The Prince and Other Writings*, ed. and trans. Wayne A. Rebhorn (New York: Barnes & Noble, 2003).

In addition to individual English translations of *The Prince*, a number of recent translations of Machiavelli's other important works are worthy of mention. Machiavelli's historical account of his native Florence may be examined in *Florentine Histories*, ed. and trans. Laura F. Banfield and Harvey C. Mansfield, Jr. (Princeton: Princeton University Press, 1988). Two good collections of Machiavelli's private correspondence are available: *The Letters of Machiavelli*, ed. and trans. Allan Gilbert (Chicago: University of Chicago Press, 1988); and the more comprehensive *Machiavelli and His Friends: Their Personal Correspondence*, ed. and trans. James B. Atkinson and David Sices (Dekalb: Northern Illinois University Press, 1996). For Machiavelli's treatise on warfare, see two different versions: *The Art of War*, trans. Ellis Farneworth and ed. Neal Wood (New York: Da Capo Press, 1965); and *Art of War*, ed. and trans. Christopher Lynch (Chicago: University of Chicago Press, 2003). Three recent versions of Machiavelli's major work on republicanism are available: *Discourses on Livy*, ed. and trans. Harvey C. Mansfield and Nathan Tarcov (Chicago: University of Chicago Press, 1996); *The Sweetness of Power: Machiavelli's 'Discourses' & Guicciardini's 'Considerations'*, ed. and trans. James B. Atkinson and David Sices (DeKalb: Northern Illinois University Press, 2002); and *Discourses on Livy*, ed. and trans. Julia Conaway Bondanella and Peter Bondanella (Oxford: Oxford University Press, 2003). For English versions of Machiavelli's comic masterpiece *The Mandrake Root*, see the previously cited *The Portable Machiavelli*, or *Five Comedies from the Italian Renaissance*, ed. and trans. Laura Giannetti and Guido Ruggiero (Baltimore: Johns Hopkins University Press, 2003).

Machiavelli's Life and Times

An indispensable guide through the mass of critical literature devoted to Machiavelli is provided in Silvio Ruffo-Fiore, *Niccolò Machiavelli: An Annotated Bibliography of Modern Criticism and Scholarship* (New York: Greenwood Press, 1990), which covers the period 1939–88. The classic Italian treatment of Machiavelli's life and career is Roberto Ridolfi's biography, translated as *The Life of Niccolò Machiavelli* (Chicago: University of Chicago Press, 1963). An unusual intellectual biography of Machiavelli, Sebastian de Grazia's *Machiavelli in Hell* (Princeton: Princeton University Press, 1989), may be read to complement Ridolfi's more traditional approach. The most recent and readable biography of Machiavelli is Maurizio Viroli's *Niccolò's Smile: A Biography of Machiavelli*, trans. Anthony Sughaar (New York: Farrar, Straus & Giroux, 2002). Many of Machiavelli's most important private letters are discussed in John M. Najemy, *Between Friends: Discourses of Power and Desire in the Machiavelli–Vettori Letters of 1513–1515* (Princeton: Princeton University Press, 1993).

Machiavelli as Political Theorist

Wading through the articles and books on Machiavelli's political theory requires a great deal of time and energy, for the bibliography is endless. Besides the guide to it by Ruffo-Fiore, a good starting-point is a two-volume anthology of critical articles and excerpts from books edited by John Dunn and Ian Harris, *Machiavelli* (Cheltenham: Elgar Reference Collection, 1997), covering writing from 1927 to 1993. Six seminal books set Machiavelli's political thought within the context of his times: A. H. Gilbert, *Machiavelli's Prince and its Forerunners: The 'Prince' As a typical Book de Regimine Principum* (Durham, NC: Duke University Press, 1938); Felix Gilbert, *Machiavelli and Guicciardini: Politics and History in Sixteenth-Century Florence* (Princeton: Princeton University Press, 1965); Rudolf von Albertini, *Firenze dalla repubblica al principato* (Turin: Einaudi, 1970); Quentin Skinner, *The Foundations of Modern Political Thought*, 2 vols. (Cambridge: Cambridge University Press, 1978); Gennaro Sasso, *Niccolò Machiavelli: Storia del suo pensiero politico* (Bologna: Il Mulino, 1980); and J. H. Hexter, *The Vision of Politics on the Eve of the Reformation: More, Machiavelli, Seyssel* (New York: Basic Books, 1973). Several anthologies devoted to Machiavelli examine a wide range of political, historical, and literary problems in his collected works: Myron P. Gilmore (ed.), *Studies on Machiavelli* (Florence: Sansoni, 1972); Anthony Parel (ed.), *The Political Calculus: Essays on Machiavelli's Philosophy* (Toronto: University of Toronto Press, 1972); Martin Fleisher (ed.), *Machiavelli and the Nature of Political Thought* (New York: Atheneum, 1972); Jean-Jacques Marchand (ed.), *Niccolò Machiavelli politico storico letterato* (Rome: Salerno, 1996); and *Cultura e scrittura di Machiavelli* (Rome: Salerno, 1998).

Numerous studies analyse Machiavelli's political theory, some emphasizing *The Prince* while others more recently have focused attention on the *Discourses on Livy*. Sir Isaiah Berlin's often-cited essay, 'The Originality of Machiavelli', may be found in his *Against the Current* (New York: Viking Press, 1980). A quick introduction to Machiavelli may be found in Quentin Skinner's *Machiavelli: A Very Short Introduction* (Oxford: Oxford University Press, 2000). Most books on Machiavelli, however, are far more polemical, as discussing Machiavelli seems to lend itself to impassioned arguments over the meaning of his writings. Leo Strauss, *Thoughts on Machiavelli* (Seattle: University of Washington Press, 1967), still continues to provoke debate and inspire partisanship. Mark Hulliung's *Citizen Machiavelli* (Princeton: Princeton University Press, 1988) and Anthony J. Parel's *The Machiavellian Cosmos* (New Haven, Conn.: Yale University Press, 1992) both make contributions to the discussion of Machiavelli's views on citizenship, the state, and the philosophical assumptions underlying his political theory. Maurizo Viroli's *Machiavelli* (Oxford: Oxford University Press, 1998) makes a convincing argument that Machiavelli's works were composed according to the classical rules of rhetoric and were never intended to found a modern 'science of politics' as many contemporary scholars contend. See also Viroli's *From Politics to Reason of State* (Cambridge: Cambridge University Press, 1992). Roger D. Masters has argued for an important relationship between Machiavelli's political thought and Leonardo da Vinci in two books: *Fortune is a River: Leonardo da Vinci and Niccolò Machiavelli's Magnificent Dream to Change the Course of Florentine History* (New York: The Free Press, 1998), and *Machiavelli, Leonardo, and the Science of Power* (Notre Dame: University of Notre Dame Press, 1996). A feminist perspective on Machiavelli's theory is provided by Hanna Pitkin, *Fortune Is a Woman: Gender and Politics in the Thought of Machiavelli* (Berkeley: University of California Press, 1984).

Studies emphasizing Machiavelli's contributions to the history of republican thought have become more numerous in recent years, reflecting the growing critical consensus about his many positive contributions to republican theory in the *Discourses on Livy*. For a general consideration of the place of Machiavelli in the development of republican theory or in the growth of the myth of the Roman republic from the Renaissance to the present, see William R. Everdell, *The End of Kings: A History of Republics and Republicans* (New York: The Free Press, 1983); Peter Bondanella, *The Eternal City: Roman Images in the Modern World* (Chapel Hill: University of North Carolina Press, 1987); and Maurizio Viroli, *Republicanism* (New York: Hill & Wang, 2002). Machiavelli's views on ancient Rome are analysed in Vickie B. Sullivan, *Machiavelli's Three Romes: Religion, Human Liberty, and Politics Reformed* (Dekalb: Northern Illinois University Press, 1996); and J. Patrick Coby, *Machiavelli's Romans: Liberty and Greatness in the 'Discourses on Livy'* (Lanham, Md.: Lexington Books, 1999). Harvey Mansfield, Jr., *Machiavelli's New Modes and Orders* (Ithaca, NY: Cornell University Press, 1979), provides a close commentary on each book and chapter of the *Discourses on Livy*, while Mansfield's *Machiavelli's Virtue* (Chicago: University of Chicago Press, 1996) discusses not only Machiavelli's republican theory but all of his major works. A series of essays on the composition of *Discourses on Livy* by Felix Gilbert may be found in his *History: Choice and Commitment* (Cambridge, Mass.: Harvard University Press, 1977). The previously mentioned *Firenze dalla repubblica al principato* by von Albertini, and John A. G. Pocock's *The Machiavellian Moment: Florentine Political Thought and the Atlantic Republican Tradition* (Princeton: Princeton University

Press, 1975), are influential studies of Machiavelli's place within republican theory. Important essays on Machiavelli's republicanism are edited by Gisela Bock, Quentin Skinner, and Maurizio Viroli in *Machiavelli and Republicanism* (Cambridge: Cambridge University Press, 1990).

Machiavelli as a Stylist

Machiavelli's development as a historical writer from the early diplomatic correspondence to the mature historical and political works is traced by Peter Bondanella in *Machiavelli and the Art of Renaissance History* (Detroit: Wayne State University Press, 1973). Wayne A. Rebhorn's *Foxes and Lions: Machiavelli's Confidence Men* (Ithaca, NY: Cornell University Press, 1988) discusses how literary tradition informs all of Machiavelli's writings. Two recent anthologies on Machiavelli's literary works and their relationship to his political and historical writings are Albert Ascoli and Victoria Kahn (eds.), *Machiavelli and the Discourse of Literature* (Ithaca, NY: Cornell University Press, 1993); and Vickie B. Sullivan (ed.), *The Comedy and Tragedy of Machiavelli: Essays on the Literary Works* (New Haven, Conn.: Yale University Press, 2000). The previously cited *Machiavelli* by Maurizio Viroli provides much information about Machiavelli's place in the rhetorical tradition. In Italian, the best discussion of Machiavelli's theatre is Ezio Raimondi's *Politica e commedia* (Bologna: Il Mulino, 1972).

Machiavelli's Influence

The impact of Machiavelli's work upon subsequent generations of writers, philosophers, historians, and politicians may be traced in a number of works: Friedrich Meinecke, *Machiavellism: The Doctrine of Raison d'etat and Its Place in Modern History* (New Haven, Conn.: Yale University Press, 1957); Felix Raab, *The English Face of Machiavelli: A Changing Interpretation 1500–1700* (London: Routledge & Kegan Paul, 1964); Josef Macek, *Machiavelli e il Machiavellismo* (Florence: La Nuova Italian, 1980); Giuliano Procacci, *Machiavelli nella cultura europea dell'età moderna* (Rome: Laterza, 1995); *La virtù e la libertà: Ideali e civiltà nella formazione degli Stati Uniti*, ed. Marcello Pacini (Turin: Edizioni della Fondazione Giovanni Agnelli, 1995); and Victoria Kahn, *Machiavellian Rhetoric from the Counter-Reformation to Milton* (Princeton: Princeton University Press, 1994).

Recent interpretations of Machiavelli have examined his works for advice about both political leadership and corporate management. Michael A. Ledeen's *Machiavelli on Modern Leadership: Why Machiavelli's Iron Rules Are as Timely and Important as Five Centuries Ago* (New York: St Martin's Press, 2000), and Keith Grint's edition of readings on *Leadership: Classical, Contemporary, and Critical Approaches* (Oxford: Oxford University Press, 1997) are excellent examples of recent approaches to Machiavelli as a guide to contemporary political practice. James Burnham's *The Machiavellians: Defenders of Freedom* (New York: John Day, 1943) began the use of Machiavelli as a model for managerial behaviour, followed by the bestseller of John Jay, *Management and Machiavelli: Discovering a New Science of Management in the Timeless Principles of Statecraft* (Oxford: Pfeiffer, 1997; original edn. 1968). One very useful collection of essays dealing with Machiavelli as a model for business practices is *Machiavelli, Marketing and Management*, ed. Phil Harris, Andrew Lock, and Patricia Rees (London: Routledge, 2000). Other books on Machiavelli and management include: Richard W. Hill, *The Boss: Machiavelli on Managerial Leadership* (New York: Pyramid, 2000); Alistair McAlpine, *The New Machiavelli: The Art of Politics in Business* (New York: Wiley, 2000); Stanley Bing, *What Would Machiavelli Do? The Ends Justify the Meanness* (New York: Harper, 2000); and Ian Demack, *The Modern Machiavelli: Power and Influence at Work* (Warriewood, Australia: Business + Publishing, 2001). Less serious applications of Machiavelli's ideas to human behaviour may be examined in the following books: Harriet Rubin: *The Princessa: Machiavelli for Women* (New York: Dell, 1997); V., *The Mafia Manager: The Guide to the Corporate Machiavelli* (New York: St Martin's Press, 1997); Nick Casanova, *The Machiavellian's Guide to Womanizing* (Edison, NJ: Castle, 1999); and Claudia Hart, *A Child's Machiavelli: A Primer on Power* (New York: Penguin Studio, 1998).

Further Reading in Oxford World's Classics

Ariosto, Ludovico, *Orlando furioso*, trans. Guido Waldman.

Cellini, Benvenuto, *My Life*, trans. Julia Conaway Bondanella and Peter Bondanella.

Cicero, *The Republic and The Laws*, trans. Niall Rudd, ed. Jonathan Powell.

Michelangelo, *Life, Letters, and Poetry*, trans. George Bull and Peter Porter.

Three Early Modern Utopias, ed. Susan Bruce.

Vasari, Giorgio, *The Lives of the Artists*, trans. Julia Conaway Bondanella and Peter Bondanella.

A CHRONOLOGY OF NICCOLÒ MACHIAVELLI

1469   Niccolò di Bernardo Machiavelli is born in Florence.

1498   Machiavelli is appointed and subsequently elected to head the Second Chancery of the Republic of Florence; shortly thereafter he receives an additional post as Secretary to the Ten of Liberty and Peace. He is regarded as the confidant of Pier Soderini, Gonfaloniere or Standard-bearer of Florence, the chief executive officer of the Florentine Republic.

1500   Completes his first diplomatic mission to France, meeting King Louis XII and Georges d'Amboise, cardinal of Rouen.

1502–3   Completes diplomatic missions to Cesare Borgia in the Romagna and Rome, witnessing Borgia's fall from power after the death of his father, Pope Alexander VI.

1504   Returns to Florence.

1506   Is sent on a diplomatic mission by the republic to Pope Julius II.

1507–8   Undertakes his first mission to Emperor Maximilian.

1512   Soderini's republic is overthrown and the Medici return to power in Florence.

1513   Dismissed from office and tortured, Machiavelli retires to his country place in Sant'Andrea in Percussina and begins the *Discourses on Livy*; he completes *The Prince*.

1513–17   Completes *Discourses on Livy*.

1515–16 (?)   *The Art of War* is completed.

1518 (?)   Composes a comedy entitled *The Mandrake Root*, his greatest literary work.

1519 (?)   The first edition of *The Mandrake Root* appears, the first published work by Machiavelli.

1520   After writing *The Life of Castruccio Castracani*, the archetypal biography of an ideal prince, Machiavelli receives a commission to write a history of Florence from the then Cardinal Giulio de' Medici (later Pope Clement VII).

1521   *The Art of War* is published, the only one of Machiavelli's political or historical works to appear in print during his lifetime.

1525   *Clizia*, another comedy, is staged; Machiavelli also probably composed his *Discourse or Dialogue on Language*, although the work's authorship is disputed.

1526   *Florentine Histories* is presented to Pope Clement VII in manuscript.

1527   Machiavelli dies and is buried in Santa Croce in Florence.

1531   Posthumous publication of the *Discourses on Livy*.

1532   Posthumous publication of *The Prince*.

1559   Machiavelli's collected works are placed on the Index of Prohibited Books.

1640   The first English translation of *The Prince*, by Edward Dacres, appears.

Northern and central Italy, *c.*1500

Niccolò Machiavelli
Of Principalities
To the Magnificent Lorenzo de' Medici

[*Nicolai Maclavelli*
De principatibus
Ad magnificum Laurentium Medicem]

CONTENTS

DEDICATORY LETTER

Niccolò Machiavelli to
the Magnificent Lorenzo de' Medici*

*[Nicolaus Maclavellus magnifico Laurentiio Medici
iuniori salutem*]*

IN most instances it is customary for those who desire to win the
favour of a prince to present themselves to him along with those
things which they value most or which they feel will most please
him.* Thus, we often see princes given horses, arms, and vest-
ments of gold cloth, precious stones, and similar ornaments
suited to their greatness.* Wishing, therefore, to offer myself to
Your Magnificence with some evidence of my devotion to you, I
have not found among my belongings anything that I might value
more or prize so much as the knowledge of the deeds of great
men that I have learned from a long experience in modern affairs
and a continuous study of antiquity.* Having with great care and
for a long time thought about and examined these deeds, and
having now set them down in a little book, I am sending them to
Your Magnificence. And although I consider this work unworthy
of your station, nevertheless I am sure that your humanity will
move you to accept it, for there could not be a greater gift from
me than to give you the means to be able, in a very short time, to
understand all that in so many years and with so many hardships
and dangers I have come to understand and to appreciate. I have
neither decorated nor filled this work with elaborate sentences,
with rich and magnificent words, or with any other form of rhetorical or unnecessary ornamentation that many writers normally
use in describing and enriching their subject-matter, for I wished
that nothing should set my work apart or make it pleasing except
the variety of its material and the gravity of its contents.* Neither
do I wish that it be thought presumptuous if a man of low and
inferior social condition dares to examine and lay down rules for
the governance of princes. For just as those who paint landscapes

place themselves in a low position on the plain in order to consider the nature of the mountains and the heights, and place themselves high on top of mountains in order to study the plains, in like manner, to know the nature of the people well one must be a prince, and to know the nature of princes well one must be of the people.

Accept, therefore, Your Magnificence, this little gift in the spirit that I send it. If you read and consider it carefully, you will discover in it my most heartfelt desire that you may attain the greatness that Fortune* and all your own qualities promise you. And if Your Magnificence will at some time turn your eyes from the summit of your high position toward these low places, you will realize to what degree I unjustly suffer a great and continuous malignity of Fortune.*

I

How many kinds of principalities there are and the ways they are acquired

[Quot sint genera principatuum et quibus modis acquirantur]

ALL states and all dominions that have had and continue to have power over men have been, and still are, either republics or principalities.* Principalities are either hereditary, in which instance the family of the prince has ruled for generations, or they are new.* The new ones are either completely new, as was Milan for Francesco Sforza,* or they are like appendages added to the hereditary state of the prince who acquires them, as is the Kingdom of Naples for the King of Spain.* Dominions taken in this way are either accustomed to living under a prince or are used to being free; and they are gained either by the arms of others or by one's own, either through Fortune or through virtue.*

Republican leanings. Cannot be free in principality

II

Of hereditary principalities

[De principatibus hereditariis]

I SHALL set aside any discussion of republics, because I have treated them at length elsewhere.* I shall consider solely the principality, weaving together the threads mentioned above as I go, and I shall discuss how these principalities can be governed and maintained.

I say, then, that in hereditary states accustomed to the rule of their prince's family, there are far fewer difficulties in maintaining them than in new states, for it is sufficient simply not to break ancient customs, and then to suit one's actions to unexpected events. In this way, if such a prince is of ordinary ability he will always maintain his state, unless some extraordinary and

inertia

Contrast w/ Alberti certain that undistinguished leaders will squander riches inordinate force should deprive him of it, and although it may be taken away from him, he will regain it at the slightest mistake of the usurper.

As an example, we have in Italy the Duke of Ferrara,* who withstood the assaults of the Venetians in 1484 and those of Pope Julius in 1510 for no other reason than his long-established rule in that dominion. Because a prince by birth has fewer reasons and less need to harm his subjects, it is natural that he should be more loved; and if no unusual vices make him hated, it is reasonable that he should be naturally well liked by them. And through the great length and continuity of his dominion the memories and causes of innovations die out, because one change always leaves indentations for the construction of another.*

III

Of mixed principalities

[*De principatibus mixtis*]

But it is in the new principality that difficulties arise. In the first place, if it is not completely new but is like an added appendage (so that the two parts together may be called mixed), its difficulties derive first from one natural problem inherent in all new principalities: that men gladly change their ruler, thinking to better themselves. This belief causes them to take up arms against their ruler, but they fool themselves in this, since they then see through experience that matters have become worse. This stems from another natural and ordinary necessity, which is that a new prince must always harm his new subjects, both with his soldiers as well as with countless other injuries involved in his new conquest. Thus, you have made enemies of all those you harmed in occupying the principality, and you are unable to maintain as friends those who helped you to rise to power, since you cannot satisfy them in the way that they had supposed. Nor can you use strong medicines* against them, for you are in their debt: this is so because, although someone may have the most powerful of

armies, he always needs the support of the inhabitants to seize a
region. For these reasons, Louis XII, King of France, quickly
occupied Milan and just as quickly lost it.* The first time, the
troops of Ludovico alone were needed to retake it from him,
because those citizens who had opened the gates of the city to the
King, finding themselves deceived in their beliefs and in that
future improvement they had anticipated, could not support the
vexations of the new prince.

It is indeed true that when lands that have rebelled once are
taken a second time it is more difficult to lose them; for the ruler,
taking advantage of the rebellion, is less reticent about punishing
offenders, ferreting out suspects, and shoring up weak positions.
And so, if only a Duke Ludovico* creating a border disturbance
sufficed for France to lose Milan the first time, the whole world*
had to oppose her and destroy her armies or chase them from
Italy to cause her to lose it the second time. This occurred for the
reasons mentioned above. Nevertheless, it was taken from her
both the first and the second time. The general explanations for
the first loss have been discussed. Now it remains to specify those
for the second, and to see what remedies the King of France had,
and those that someone in the same situation could have, so as to
be able to maintain a stronger grip on his conquest than France
did.

I say, therefore, that those dominions, upon being conquered
and added to the long-established state of the one who acquires
them, are either of the same region and language or they are not.
When they are it is easier to hold them, especially when they are
unaccustomed to freedom. To possess them securely it is sufficient only to have wiped out the family line of the prince who
ruled them, because so far as other things are concerned, men live
peacefully as long as their old way of life is maintained and there
is no change in customs. We have seen what happened in the case
of Burgundy, Brittany, Gascony, and Normandy,* which have
been part of France for such a long time; and although there are
some linguistic differences, nevertheless the customs are similar,
and they have been able to get along together easily. Anyone who
acquires these lands and wishes to hold on to them must keep two

things in mind: first, that the family line of the old prince must be wiped out; second, that neither their laws nor their taxes be altered. As a result, in a very short time they will become one body with the old principality.

But when dominions are acquired in a region that is not similar in language, customs, and institutions, it is here that difficulties arise; and it is here that one needs much good luck and much diligence to hold on to them. One of the best and most efficacious remedies would be for the person who has taken possession of them to go there to live. This would make that possession more secure and durable; as happened with the Turk in Greece;* for despite all the other methods he employed to retain that dominion, if he had not gone to live there it would have been impossible for him to hold on to it. By being on the spot, troubles are seen at their birth and can be quickly remedied; not being there, they are heard about after they have grown up and there is no longer any remedy. Moreover, the region would not be plundered by your own officers; the subjects would be pleased to have direct recourse to their prince; thus, those wishing to be good subjects have more reason to love him, and those wanting to be otherwise, more reason to fear him. Anyone who might wish to invade that dominion from abroad would be more hesitant; so that living right there, it is only with the greatest difficulty that the prince can lose it.

The other and better solution is to send colonies into one or two places, that will act as shackles* on that state; for it is necessary that the prince either do this or maintain a large number of cavalry and infantry. Colonies do not cost much, and with little or no expense a prince can send and maintain them. In so doing he injures only those whose fields and houses have been taken away and given to the new inhabitants, who are only a small part of that dominion. Those he injures, finding themselves scattered and poor, can never be a threat to him; and all the others remain uninjured on the one hand, and because of this they should remain peaceful, and on the other hand are afraid of making a mistake, for fear that what happened to those who were dispossessed might happen to them. I conclude that these colonies are not expensive, they are more loyal, they are less injurious, and the offended can do no harm since they are poor and scattered (as I have said). Concerning this, it should be noted that men must be either caressed or wiped out; because they will avenge minor injuries, but cannot do so for grave ones. Any harm done to a man must be of the kind that removes any fear of revenge. But by garrisoning troops there instead of colonies, one spends much more, being obliged to consume all the revenues of the state in standing guard, so that the gain turns into a loss; and far greater injury is committed, since the entire state is harmed by the army changing quarters from one place to another. Everybody resents this inconvenience, and everyone becomes the ruler's enemy; and these are enemies that can be harmful, since, although conquered, they remain in their own homes. And so, in every respect, this form of protection is as useless as the other kind, colonization, is useful.

Moreover, anyone who is in a region that is unlike his own in the ways mentioned above should make himself the leader and defender of his less powerful neighbours, and do all he can to weaken those who are more powerful; and he should be careful that, for whatever reason, no foreigner equal to himself in strength should enter there. And it will always happen that the outsider will be brought in by those who are dissatisfied, either because of too much ambition or because of fear, as was once seen when the Aetolians brought the Romans into Greece.* In every other province that the Romans entered, the native inhabitants brought them in. The order of things is such that, as soon as a powerful foreigner enters a region, all who are less powerful cling to him, moved by the envy they have against the ruler who has ruled over them. And so, concerning these weaker powers, the invader has no trouble whatsoever in winning them over, since all of them will immediately and willingly become part of the state he has acquired. He need only be careful that they do not seize too much military power and authority. With his own military power and their support, he can very easily put down those who are powerful, and remain complete arbiter of that region. Anyone who does not follow this procedure will quickly lose what he has taken, and while he holds it, he will find it full of infinite difficulties and troubles.

In the regions they conquered the Romans followed these rules very carefully. They sent out colonies, had dealings with the less powerful without increasing their strength, put down the powerful, and did not allow powerful foreigners to gain prestige there. I shall cite only the region of Greece as an example: the Romans kept the Achaeans and the Aetolians in check; they put down the Kingdom of Macedon;* Antiochus was driven out.* Nor did they ever permit the Achaeans or the Aetolians to expand their territory, despite their merits. Nor did the persuasion of Philip of Macedon ever convince them to make him their friend without first humbling him. Nor could the power of Antiochus force their consent to his having any dominion whatsoever in that region. For the Romans did in these instances what all wise princes must do: they must be on their guard not only against existing dangers but also against future disturbances, and try diligently to prevent them. Once evils are recognized ahead of time, they may be easily cured; but if you wait for them to come upon you, the medicine will be too late, because the disease will have become incurable. And what physicians say about consumptive illnesses* is applicable here: that at the beginning, such an illness is easy to cure but difficult to diagnose; but as time passes, not having been recognized or treated at the outset, it becomes easy to diagnose but difficult to cure. The same thing occurs in affairs of state; by recognizing evils in advance (a gift granted only to the prudent ruler), they can be cured quickly; but when they are not recognized and are left to grow to such an extent that everyone recognizes them, there is no longer any remedy.

Thus, recognizing dangers from afar, the Romans always found remedies for them; and they never allowed them to develop in order to avoid a war, because they knew that war cannot be avoided, but can only be put off to the advantage of others. Therefore, they wanted to go to war with Philip and Antiochus in Greece in order not to have to face them in Italy; and at the time, they could have avoided both the one and the other, but they did not want to do so. Nor did they ever approve of what is always on the lips of our wise men today—to reap the benefits of time. Instead, they reaped the benefits of their virtue and prudence; for time brings with it all things, and it can bring with it the good as well as the evil, and the evil as well as the good.

But let us return to France, and observe whether she did any of the things we have just mentioned. I shall speak of Louis and not of Charles;* and therefore about the one whose progress has been observed better, because he held territory in Italy for a longer period. You will see that he did the contrary of those things that must be done in order to hold one's dominion in a region with heterogeneous customs, languages, and institutions. King Louis was brought into Italy because of the ambition of the Venetians,* who wanted by his coming to gain for themselves half of Lombardy. I have no wish to criticize the decision the King made. Wishing to establish a first foothold in Italy, and not having any friends in this region, and furthermore, having all the gates closed to him because of the actions of King Charles,* he was forced to strike up whatever alliances he could. This laudable decision would have succeeded if he had not erred in his other moves. After having taken Lombardy, then, the King immediately regained the reputation that Charles had lost him: Genoa surrendered;* the Florentines became his allies;* the Marquis of Mantua, the Duke of Ferrara, the Bentivoglios, the Countess of Forlì, the rulers of Faenza, Rimini, Pesaro, Camerino, and Piombino, as well as the people of Lucca, Pisa, and Siena, all rushed to become his ally.* At this point the Venetians could understand the recklessness of the decision they had taken. To acquire two towns in Lombardy, they had made the King master of two-thirds of Italy.*

Consider now, first, with what little difficulty the King might have maintained his reputation in Italy if he had followed the above-mentioned rules and kept secure and defended all those allies of his who, being numerous but both weak and fearful— some afraid of the Church, others afraid of the Venetians—were always forced to remain his allies; and with their assistance, he could have easily protected himself against the remaining greater powers. But no sooner was he in Milan than he did the opposite, providing assistance to Pope Alexander so that he could occupy the Romagna. Nor did he realize that with this decision he had made himself weaker, abandoning his allies and those who had thrown themselves into his lap, and he had made the Church stronger by adding to it so much temporal power, in addition to the spiritual power from which it derives so much authority. Having committed this first error, he was obliged to continue,* so that in order to put an end to the ambition of Alexander and to keep him from becoming the ruler of Tuscany,* the King was forced to invade Italy.

It was not enough for him to have made the Church powerful and to have alienated his allies, for since he coveted the Kingdom of Naples, he divided it with the King of Spain. And whereas previously he had been the arbiter of Italy, he now brought in a partner, so that the ambitious and the malcontented of that region had someone else to whom they could turn for help. And whereas he could have left a tributary king to rule that kingdom, Louis replaced him,* establishing one there who could, in turn, drive Louis out. The desire to gain possessions is truly a very natural and normal thing, and when those men gain possessions who are able to do so, they will always be praised and not criticized. But when they are not able to do so, and yet wish to do so at any cost, therein lie the error and the blame. Therefore, if France could have attacked Naples with her own troops, she should have done so. If she could not, she should not have shared it. And if the sharing of Lombardy with the Venetians deserves to be excused, since it allowed Louis to gain a foothold in Italy, this other sharing deserves to be criticized, since it cannot be excused by necessity.

Thus, Louis committed these five errors he wiped out the less powerful rulers; he increased the power of an already powerful ruler in Italy; he brought into that region an extremely powerful foreigner; he did not go there to live; and he did not set up colonies there. In spite of all this, these errors (had he lived) might not have injured him if he had not made a sixth: that of reducing the dominion of the Venetians.* For if he had not made the Church stronger, nor brought Spain into Italy, it would have been most reasonable and necessary to put the Venetians down; but, having made those first decisions, he should never have agreed to their ruin, for as long as the Venetians were powerful they would have always kept the others from trying to seize Lombardy, partly because the Venetians would not have allowed this unless they themselves became the rulers of Lombardy, and partly because the others would not have wanted to take it away from France to give it to the Venetians; and they would not have had the nerve to attack both France and Venice.

And if someone were to say that King Louis handed over the Romagna to Alexander and the Kingdom of Naples to Spain in order to avoid a war, I would reply with the arguments advanced above: that one should never allow disorder to persist in order to avoid going to war, because one does not avoid a war but, instead, defers it to your disadvantage. And if some others were to bring forward as evidence the promise that the King made the Pope, to undertake that enterprise in return for the annulment of his marriage and the cardinal's hat for the Archbishop of Rouen,* I would reply with what I shall say later about the promises of princes and how they should be observed.*

King Louis lost Lombardy, therefore, by not following any of the precepts observed by others who seized territories and wished to retain them. Nor is this in any sense a miracle, but very ordinary and to be expected. I spoke about this at Nantes* with the Cardinal of Rouen, when Valentino (as Cesare Borgia, son of Pope Alexander, was commonly called)* was capturing the Romagna. When the Cardinal of Rouen told me that Italians understood little about warfare, I replied to him that the French understood little about statecraft, for if they had some understanding, they would not have permitted the Church to gain so much power. Experience has shown that the power of both the Church and of Spain in Italy has been caused by France, and that her downfall has been brought about by the Church and by Spain. From this one can derive a general rule which rarely, if ever, fails: that anyone who is the cause of another becoming powerful comes to ruin himself; because that power has been brought about by him either through cunning or by force; and both of these two qualities are suspect to the one who has become powerful.

the adversary [handwritten]

Relate to decentralisation of power [handwritten]

IV

Why the kingdom of Darius, occupied by Alexander, did not rebel against his successors after the death of Alexander

[*Cur Darii regnum, quod Alexander occupaverat, a successoribus suis post Alexandri mortem non defecit*]

CONSIDERING the difficulties one has in maintaining a newly acquired territory, one might wonder how it happened that when Alexander the Great died, having become ruler of Asia in a few years and having hardly occupied it, Alexander's successors* nevertheless managed to hold on to it, although it would have seemed reasonable for the whole region to revolt. And in keeping it, they had no other difficulty than that which arose among themselves from their own ambition. Let me reply that all principalities known to us are governed in two different ways: either by a prince with all the others his servants, who as ministers (through his favour and permission) assist in governing that kingdom; or by a prince and by barons, who hold that rank not because of any favour of their master but because of the antiquity of their bloodline. Such barons as these have their own dominions and subjects, who recognize them as masters and have natural affection for them. In those states that are governed by a prince and his servants, the prince has greater authority, for in all his territories there is no one else recognized as superior to him; and if the people do obey any other persons, it is because they are his ministers and officials; and they harbour a special affection for him.

Contemporary examples of these two different kinds of governments are the Turk and the King of France. One ruler governs the entire kingdom of the Turk; the others are his servants; and

dividing his kingdom into sanjaks,* he sends various adminis-
trators there, and he moves them and changes them around as he
pleases. But the King of France is placed among a group of
hereditary nobles who are recognized in that state by their subjects and who are loved by them; they have their hereditary
privileges, which the King cannot take away without endanger-
ing himself. Anyone, then, who considers the one and the other of
these two states will find that for the Turk the difficulty lies in
taking possession of the state, but once it has been conquered it is
very simple to hold on to it. And so (on the other hand), you will
find that in some respects it is easier to occupy the Kingdom of
France, but extremely difficult to hold on to it.

The reasons for the difficulty in being able to occupy the kingdom of the Turk are because it is not possible to be summoned
there by the princes of that kingdom, or to hope, through the
rebellion of those the ruler has around him, to make your enterprise easier. This is because of the reasons mentioned above: since
they are all his slaves and bound to him, it is more difficult to
corrupt them; and even if they could be corrupted, little profit
can be hoped for, since they will not be followed by the people for
the reasons already discussed. Therefore, anyone who attacks the
Turk must realize that he will find him completely united, and he
must rely more on his own forces than on the disunity of his
opponent. But once beaten and broken in battle so that he cannot
regroup his troops, there is nothing else to be feared than the
ruler's family. Once it has been wiped out, there remains no one
else to be feared, for the others have no credit with the people.
And just as, before the victory, the victor could place no hope in
them, so afterwards he should not fear them.

The opposite occurs in kingdoms governed like that of France,
because you can invade them with ease once you have won to your
side some barons of the kingdom, since you can always find
malcontents and men who desire a change. These people, for the
reasons already given, can open the way to that dominion and
facilitate your victory. However, when you wish to hold on to it
this is accompanied by endless problems, both with those who
have helped you and with those you have suppressed. Nor is it

sufficient for you to wipe out the ruling family, since the nobles who make themselves heads of new insurrections still remain. And since you are neither able to make them happy nor to wipe them out, you lose that dominion whenever the opportunity arises.

Now, if you will consider the type of government Darius had, you will find it similar to the kingdom of the Turk; and therefore Alexander had first to overwhelm it totally and defeat it in battle. After this victory, Darius being dead, that state remained securely in Alexander's hands for the reasons discussed above. And had his successors been united they would have enjoyed it at their leisure, for in that kingdom no disorders arose other than those they stirred up themselves. But in states organized like that of France, it is impossible to hold them with such tranquillity. Because of this there arose the frequent rebellions in Spain, France, and Greece against the Romans, all because of the numerous principalities that existed in those regions. So long as the memory of them lasted, Rome was always uncertain of those possessions; but once this memory had been wiped out because of their long and powerful rule, the Romans became sure possessors. Afterwards, when the Romans fought among themselves, each Roman leader was able to draw a following from those regions, according to the authority he enjoyed there, and since the bloodlines of their former rulers had been wiped out, these regions acknowledged only the Romans. Taking all these things into account, therefore, no one should be at all surprised by the ease with which Alexander held on to the region of Asia, or by the problems others encountered in preserving the territory they acquired, such as Pyrrhus and many others. This is not caused by the greater or lesser virtue of the conqueror, but rather by the different characteristics of the conquered territories.

V

How cities or principalities should be governed that lived by their own laws before they were occupied

[Quodmodo administrande sunt civitates vel principatus qui ante quam occuparentur suis legibus vivebant]

WHEN those states that are acquired, as I have said, are accustomed to living under their own laws and in freedom, there are three methods of holding on to them: the first is to destroy them; the second is to go there in person to live; the third is to allow them to live with their own laws, forcing them to pay a tribute and creating an oligarchy there that will keep the state friendly toward you.* For since such a government, having been set up by that prince, knows it cannot last without his friendship and power, it must do everything possible to maintain them. A city accustomed to living in freedom is more easily maintained through the means of its own citizens than in any other way, if you decide to preserve it.

As examples, there are the Spartans and the Romans. The Spartans held Athens and Thebes by establishing oligarchies there;* yet they lost them both. In order to hold Capua, Carthage, and Numantia, the Romans destroyed them and did not lose them.* They wished to hold Greece in almost the same manner as the Spartans held it, making it free and leaving it under its own laws, and they did not succeed. Thus, they were obliged to destroy many of the cities in that region in order to retain it.* For in fact, there is no secure means of holding on to cities except by destroying them. Anyone who becomes master of a city accustomed to living in liberty and does not destroy it may expect to be destroyed by it, because such a city always has as a refuge in any rebellion the name of liberty and its ancient institutions, neither of which is ever forgotten either because of the passing of time or because of the bestowal of benefits. And it matters very little what one does or foresees, since if one does not separate or scatter the inhabitants, they will not forget that name or those institutions. Immediately, and in every instance, they will return to them, just as Pisa did * after one hundred years of being held in servitude by the Florentines. However, when cities or regions are accustomed to living under a prince and his bloodline has been wiped out, being on the one hand accustomed to obedience and, on the other, not having their old prince and not being able to agree upon choosing another one from amongst themselves—yet not knowing how to live as free men—they are, as a result, hesitant in taking up arms, and a prince can win them over and assure himself of their support with greater ease. But in republics, greater vitality, greater hatred, and greater desire for revenge exist. The memory of ancient liberty does not and cannot allow them to rest, so that the most secure course is either to wipe them out or to go to live there.

VI

Of new principalities acquired by one's own troops and virtue

[*De principatibus novis qui armis propriis et virtute acquiruntur*]

No one should wonder if, in speaking of principalities that are completely new as to their ruler and form of government, I cite the greatest examples. Since men almost always follow the paths trod by others, and proceed in their affairs by imitation,* although they are not fully able to stay on the path of others, nor to equal the virtue of those they imitate, a wise man should always enter those paths trodden by great men, and imitate those who have been most excellent, so that if one's own virtue does not match theirs, at least it will have the smell of it. He should do as those prudent archers do* who, aware of the strength of their bow when the target at which they are aiming seems too distant, set their sights much higher than the designated target, not in order to reach such a height with their arrow, but instead to be able, by aiming so high, to strike their target.

I say, therefore, that in completely new principalities, where there is a new prince, greater or lesser difficulty in maintaining them exists according to the greater or lesser virtue of the person who acquires them. Because for a private citizen to become a prince presupposes virtue or Fortune, it appears that either the one or the other of these two things should partially mitigate many of the problems. Nevertheless, he who relies less upon Fortune has maintained his position best. Matters are also facilitated when the prince, having no other dominions to govern, is constrained to come to live there in person.

However, to come to those who have become princes by means of their own virtue and not because of Fortune, I say that the most outstanding are Moses, Cyrus, Romulus, Theseus, and others of their kind.* Although we should not discuss Moses, since he was a mere executor of things he was ordered to do by God, nevertheless he must be admired at least for the grace that made him worthy of speaking with God. Let us then consider Cyrus and the others who have acquired or founded kingdoms. You will find them all admirable; and if their deeds and their particular methods are considered, they will not appear different from those of Moses, who had so great a teacher. In examining their deeds and their lives, one can see that they received nothing from Fortune except opportunity, which gave them the material they could mould into whatever form they liked.* Without that opportunity the strength of their spirit would have been exhausted, and without that strength, their opportunity would have come in vain.

It was therefore necessary for Moses to find the people of Israel slaves in Egypt and oppressed by the Egyptians, in order that they might be disposed to follow him to escape this servitude. It was necessary for Romulus not to stay in Alba, and that he be exposed at birth, so that he might become king of Rome and founder of that nation. It was necessary for Cyrus to find the Persians unhappy about the rule of the Medes, and the Medes rendered soft and effeminate after a lengthy peace. Theseus could not have demonstrated his ability if he had not found the Athenians dispersed. These opportunities, therefore, made these

[handwritten: Cunning & perspicacity are praised as high virtues — different then heroic or shrewdness?]

men successful, and their outstanding virtue enabled them to recognize that opportunity,* whereby their nation was ennobled and became extremely happy.

Those who, like these men, become princes through their virtue acquire the principality with difficulty, but they hold on to it easily. The difficulties they encounter in acquiring the principality grow, in part, out of the new institutions and methods* they are forced to introduce in order to establish their state and their security. One should bear in mind that there is nothing more difficult to execute, nor more dubious of success, nor more dangerous to administer, than to introduce new political orders. For the one who introduces them has as his enemies all those who profit from the old order, and he has only lukewarm defenders in all those who might profit from the new order. This lukewarmness partly arises from fear of the adversaries who have the law on their side, and partly from the incredulity of men, who do not truly believe in new things unless they have actually had personal experience of them. Therefore, it happens that whenever those who are enemies have the chance to attack, they do so with partisan zeal, whereas those others defend hesitantly, so that they, together with the prince, run the risk of grave danger.

However, if we desire to examine this argument thoroughly, it is necessary to consider whether these innovators act on their own or are dependent on others: that is, if they are forced to beg for help or are able to employ force in conducting their affairs. In the first case, they always come to a bad end and never accomplish anything. But when they depend on their own resources and can use force, then only seldom do they run the risk of grave danger. From this comes the fact that all armed prophets were victorious and the unarmed came to ruin. For, besides what has been said, people are fickle by nature: it is easy to convince them of something, but difficult to hold them in that conviction. Therefore, affairs should be managed in such a way that when they no longer believe, they can be made to believe by force. Moses, Cyrus, Theseus, and Romulus could not have made their institutions respected for long if they had been unarmed; as in our times happened to Brother Girolamo Savonarola,* who was ruined in his new institutions when the populace began to believe in them no longer, since he had no way of holding steady those who had believed, nor of making the unbelievers believe.

Therefore, such men encounter serious problems in conducting their affairs, and meet all their dangers as they proceed, and must overcome them with their virtue. However, once they have overcome them and have begun to be venerated, having wiped out all those who were envious of their accomplishments, they remain powerful, secure, honoured, and successful.

To such lofty examples I should like to add a lesser one; but it will have some relation to the others, and I should like it to suffice for all similar cases: and this is Hiero of Syracuse. From a private citizen, this man became the ruler of Syracuse. He received nothing from Fortune but the opportunity, for as the citizens of Syracuse were oppressed, they elected him as their captain, and from that rank he proved himself worthy of becoming their prince. He had so much virtue while still a private citizen that someone who wrote about him said: 'quod nihil illi deerat ad regnandum praeter regnum' ['that he lacked nothing to reign but a kingdom'].* He did away with the old army and established a new one; he abandoned old alliances and forged new ones; since he possessed allies and soldiers of his own, he was able to construct whatever he desired on such a foundation; so that it cost him great effort to acquire, but little to maintain.

VII

Of new principalities acquired with the arms of others and by Fortune

[*De principatibus novis qui alienis armis et fortuna acquiruntur*]

THOSE private citizens who become princes through Fortune alone do so with little effort, but to maintain their position they need a great deal. They encounter no obstacles along their way, since they fly there, but all their problems arise once they have arrived. And these are the men who have been granted a state either because they have money, or because they enjoy the favour of him who grants it. This occurred to many in Greece, in the cities of Ionia and the Hellespont, where Darius set up rulers in order to hold these cities for his own security and glory. The same thing happened to those emperors who came to power from being private citizens by corrupting the soldiers.

Such men depend solely upon two very uncertain and unstable things: the will and the Fortune of him who granted them the state. But they do not know how, and are unable, to maintain their position. They do not know how to hold their state, since if men are not of great intelligence and virtue, it is not reasonable that they should know how to command, having always lived as private citizens. They are unable to do so, since they do not have forces that are faithful and loyal to them. Besides, states that arise quickly, just like all the other natural things that are born and grow rapidly, cannot have roots and branches and will be wiped out by the first adverse weather. This occurs unless the men who have suddenly become princes (as I have noted) possess such virtue that they know how to prepare themselves rapidly to preserve what Fortune has dropped into their laps, and to construct afterwards those foundations others have laid before becoming princes.

Regarding the two methods just mentioned for becoming a prince, by virtue or by Fortune, I should like to offer two examples from recent memory: Francesco Sforza and Cesare Borgia. Francesco became Duke of Milan from his station as a private citizen through appropriate methods and a great deal of virtue; and what he acquired with a thousand hardships he maintained with little effort. On the other hand, Cesare Borgia, called by the people Duke Valentino, acquired the state through the Fortune of his father, and when this was lost, he lost it; despite the fact that he did everything and used every method that a prudent and virtuous man ought to employ in order to root himself securely in those states that the arms and Fortune of others had granted him. For (as was stated above), anyone who does not lay his foundations beforehand can do so later only with the greatest of virtue, although this is done with difficulty for the architect and danger to the building. If, therefore, we consider all the Duke's achievements, we shall see that he laid sturdy foundations for his future power. And I do not think it useless to discuss them, since I would not know of any better precepts to give to a new prince than the example of his deeds. If he did not profit from his methods it was not his fault, but this arose from an extraordinary and extreme instance of contrary Fortune.

In his attempts to advance his son the Duke, Alexander VI. encountered many problems, both present and future. First, he saw no means of making him master of any state that was not a state of the Church. And when he decided to seize something belonging to the Church, he knew that the Duke of Milan and the Venetians would not permit this, because Faenza and Rimini were already under the protection of the Venetians. Moreover, he saw that the Italian military forces, particularly those he would have to use, were controlled by those who had reason to fear the Pope's greatness. Therefore, he could not count on them, since they all belonged to the Orsini and Colonna families or were their accomplices. It was, then, necessary to disturb the political balance of Italy and throw the Italian states into turmoil so that he could safely make himself the master of a part of them. This was easy for him to do, for he discovered that the Venetians, moved by other motives, had turned to bringing the French back into Italy. Not only did Alexander not oppose this, but he also rendered it easier by annulling King Louis's previous marriage.

The King, therefore, entered Italy with the aid of the Venetians and the consent of Alexander. No sooner was he in Milan than the Pope obtained troops from him for the Romagna campaign, and this was made possible for him because of the King's prestige. Then, having conquered the Romagna* and beaten down the Colonna,* wishing to maintain the Romagna and to advance further, the Duke was held back by two things: first, his troops, who seemed disloyal to him; and second, the will of France. That is to say, the troops of the Orsini family he had been using might let him down, and not only keep him from acquiring more territory but even take away what he had already conquered. The

The Prince

King might well do the same thing. He had one experience like this with the Orsini soldiers, when he attacked Bologna after the seizure of Faenza and saw them go reluctantly into that battle. As for the King, the Duke learned his intentions when the Duke invaded Tuscany* after the capture of the Duchy of Urbino:* the King forced him to abandon that campaign.

As a result, the Duke decided to depend no longer upon the troops and Fortune of others. His first step was to weaken the Orsini and Colonna factions in Rome. He won over all their followers who were noblemen, making them his own noblemen and giving them huge subsidies; and he honoured them, according to their rank, with military commands and civil appointments. As a result, in a few months the affection for their factions was wiped out from their hearts, and all of this affection turned towards the Duke. After this, he waited for the opportunity to wipe out the Orsini leaders, having already put to flight those of the Colonna family. A good opportunity arose, and the use he put it to was even better. For when the Orsini realized, only too late, that the greatness of the Duke and of the Church spelled their ruin, they called a meeting at Magione* in the territory of Perugia. From this resulted the rebellion of Urbino, the insurrections in the Romagna, and countless dangers for the Duke,* all of which he overcame with the assistance of the French. And when his reputation had been regained, placing no trust either in France or in other forces not his own, in order not to have to test their strength, he turned to treacherous deception. He knew how to dissimulate his intentions so well that the Orsini themselves, through Lord Paulo, reconciled themselves with him.* The Duke did not fail to employ every kind of gracious act to reassure Paulo, giving him money, garments, and horses, so that the stupidity of the Orsini brought them to Senigallia and into his clutches.*

Having wiped out these leaders,* and having reduced their partisans to his allies, the Duke had laid very good foundations for his power, possessing all of the Romagna along with the Duchy of Urbino. More important, it appeared that he had befriended the Romagna and had won the support of all of its populace once the people began to taste the beneficial results of his rule. Because this matter is worth noting and being imitated by others, I do not want to pass over it. After the Duke had taken the Romagna and had found it governed by powerless rulers— more anxious to plunder their subjects than to correct them, and who had given them reason for disunity rather than unity, so that the entire territory was full of thefts, quarrels, and every other kind of insolence—he decided that if he wanted to make the region peaceful and obedient to his regal power, it would be necessary to give it good government. Therefore, he gave a cruel and unscrupulous man, Messer Remirro de Orco, the fullest authority there. In no time at all Remirro reduced the territory to a peaceful and united state, and in so doing, the Duke greatly increased his prestige. Afterwards, the Duke judged that such excessive authority was no longer required, since he feared that it might become odious, and in the middle of the territory he set up a civil tribunal with a very distinguished president,* in which each city had its own advocate. Because he realized that the rigorous measures of the past had generated a certain amount of hatred, in order to purge the minds of the people and to win them completely over to his side he wanted to show that, if any form of cruelty had occurred, it did not originate from him but from the violent nature of his minister. Having found the occasion to do so, one morning at Cesena he had Messer Remirro's body laid out in two pieces on the piazza, with a block of wood and a bloody sword beside it. The ferocity of such a spectacle left that population satisfied and stupefied at the same time.*

But let us return to the point we digressed from. I say that the Duke, finding himself very powerful and partially secured from present dangers, having armed himself in the way he desired, and having in large measure destroyed those forces nearby that might have harmed him, still had (if he wished to continue his conquests) to take into account the King of France; for he realized that the King, who had become aware of his error only too late, would not put up with any further conquest. Because of this, he began to seek out new allies and to vacillate with France during the campaign the French undertook in the Kingdom of Naples against the Spaniards besieging Gaeta.* His intent was to make himself secure against the French, and he would have immediately succeeded in this if Alexander had lived. These were his arrangements concerning present matters.

But as for future events, he had first to fear that a new successor in control of the Church might not be his ally, and might try to take away what Alexander had given him. Against this possibility, he thought to secure himself in four ways: first, by wiping out all the bloodlines of those rulers he had despoiled in order to deprive the Pope of that opportunity; second, by gaining the friendship of all the noblemen of Rome (as mentioned already), in order to hold the Pope in check by this means; third, by making the College of Cardinals as much his own as he could; fourth, by acquiring such a large territory before the Pope died that he would be able to resist an initial attack on his own. Of these four things, he had realized three by the time of Alexander's death. The fourth he had almost realized, for he killed as many of the despoiled noblemen as he could capture, and very few saved themselves;* he had won over the Roman noblemen; he had a large faction in the College of Cardinals;* and as for the acquisition of new territory, he had plans to become ruler of Tuscany and was already in possession of Perugia and Piombino* and had taken Pisa under his protection.* As soon as he no longer needed to respect the wishes of France (for he no longer had to, since the French had already been deprived of the Kingdom of Naples by the Spaniards, forcing both of them to purchase his friendship), he would attack Pisa. After this, Lucca and Siena would have immediately surrendered, partly to spite the Florentines and partly out of fear, and the Florentines would have had no means of preventing it. If he had carried out these designs (and he would have brought them to fruition during the same year that Alexander died), he would have gathered together so many military forces and such reputation that he would have been able to stand alone and would no longer have had to rely upon the Fortune and military forces of others, but instead on his own power and virtue.

But Alexander died* five years after Cesare Borgia had drawn his sword. Alexander left his son gravely ill, with only the state of the Romagna secured and with all the others up in the air,* situated between two very powerful enemy armies.* But the Duke possessed so much ferocity and so much virtue, and so well did he understand how men can be won over or lost, and so sound were the foundations that he had laid in such a short time, that if he had not had those armies on his back or if he had been healthy, he would have surmounted every difficulty.

That his foundations were sound is witnessed by the fact that the Romagna waited more than a month for him;* in Rome, although only half alive, he was safe;* and although the Baglioni, Vitelli, and Orsini families came to Rome, they found none of their allies opposed to him. If he could not set up a pope he wanted, at least he could act to ensure that it would not be someone he did not want. If he had been healthy at the time of Alexander's demise, everything would have been simple. On the day when Julius II was made pope, he himself said to me* that he had thought about what might happen on his father's death, and had found a remedy for everything, except that he had never dreamed that at the time of his father's death he, too, would be at death's door.

Therefore, having summarized all the Duke's actions, I would not know how to reproach him. On the contrary, I believe I am correct in proposing that he be imitated by all those who have risen to power through the Fortune and with the troops of others. Possessing great courage and high goals, he could not have conducted himself in any other manner, and his plans were frustrated solely by the brevity of Alexander's life and by his own illness. Anyone, therefore, who considers it necessary in his newly acquired principality to protect himself from his enemies, to win allies, to conquer either by force or by deceit, to make himself loved and feared by the people, to be followed and revered by his soldiers, to wipe out those who can or may do you harm, to renovate ancient institutions with new ones, to be both severe and kind, magnanimous and generous, to wipe out disloyal troops and create new ones, to maintain alliances with kings and princes in such a way that they must either gladly help you or injure you with caution—that person cannot find more recent examples than this man's deeds. *what is the purpose of this praise? Is it sarastic.*

One can only reproach him for creating Julius pope, for in this he made a bad choice. For (as I said before), not being able to create a pope to suit him, he should have prevented the papacy from going to someone he did not like.* He should never have agreed to raise to the papacy any cardinal he might have injured or who, upon becoming pope, might have cause to fear him. For men do harm either out of fear or out of hatred. Those he had injured were, among others, the Cardinal of St Peter's in Chains, Cardinal Colonna, the Cardinal of San Giorgio, and Cardinal Ascanio.* Upon becoming pope, any of the others would have to fear him, except for the Cardinal of Rouen and the Spaniards— the latter because they were related to him and were in his debt, the former because of his power, since he was connected to the Kingdom of France. Therefore, above all else, the Duke should have created a Spanish pope. Failing that, he should have agreed to the election of the Cardinal of Rouen and not to that of the Cardinal of St Peter's in Chains. Anyone who believes that new benefits make men of high station forget old injuries deceives himself. The Duke, then, erred in this election, and it was the cause of his ultimate ruin.*

Kings choose Dukes' influence for interplay of temporal & divine power.

VIII

Of those who have become princes through wickedness

[*De his qui per scelera ad principatum pervenere*]

BECAUSE there still remain two additional methods for an ordinary citizen to become a prince that cannot be attributed completely to either Fortune or virtue, I believe they should not be omitted, although one of them will be discussed at greater length in a treatise on republics.* These two methods are when one becomes prince through some wicked and nefarious means; or when a private citizen becomes prince of his native city* through the favour of his fellow citizens. In discussing the first way, I shall cite two examples, one from ancient times and the other from modern times, without otherwise entering into the merits of this method, since I consider them sufficient for anyone who finds it necessary to imitate them.

Agathocles the Sicilian, who became King of Syracuse, was not only an ordinary citizen but also of the lowest and most abject condition. A potter's son, this man lived a wicked life at every stage of his career. Yet he joined to his wickedness such strength of mind and body, that when he entered upon a military career, he rose through the ranks to become praetor of Syracuse. Once placed in such a position, having decided to become prince and to hold with violence and without any obligations to others what had been conferred upon him by universal consent, and having informed Hamilcar the Carthaginian (who was waging war with his armies in Sicily), one morning he called together the people and the senate of Syracuse as if he were going to discuss some matters concerning the republic. At a prearranged signal he had his troops kill all the senators and the richest citizens; and when they were dead he seized and held the rule of the city without any opposition from the citizenry. Although he was twice defeated by the Carthaginians and finally besieged, not only was he able to defend his city, but, leaving part of his troops for the defence of the siege, with his other forces he attacked Africa, and in a short time he freed Syracuse from the siege and forced the Carthaginians into dire straits. They were obliged to make peace with him and to be content with dominion over Africa, leaving Sicily to Agathocles.*

Anyone, therefore, who examines the deeds and the life of this man will observe nothing (or very little) that can be attributed to Fortune. Not with the assistance of others (as was mentioned before), but by rising through the ranks, which involved a thousand hardships and dangers, did he come to rule the principality that he then maintained by many brave and dangerous actions. Still, it cannot be called virtue to kill one's fellow citizens, to betray allies, to be without faith, without pity, without religion; by these means one can acquire power, but not glory.* If one were to consider Agathocles' virtue in getting into and out of dangers, and his greatness of spirit in bearing up under and overcoming adversities, one can see no reason why he should be judged inferior to any most excellent commander. Nevertheless, his vicious cruelty and inhumanity, along with numerous wicked deeds, do not permit us to honour him among the most excellent of men. One cannot, therefore, attribute either to Fortune or to virtue what he accomplished without either the one or the other.

In our own days (during the reign of Alexander VI), Oliverotto of Fermo, who many years before had been left as a little child without a father, was brought up by his maternal uncle named Giovanni Fogliani. In the early days of his youth he was sent to serve as a soldier under Paulo Vitelli, so that, once he was versed in that discipline, he might attain some outstanding military rank. Then, after Paulo died,* he soldiered under Paulo's brother Vitellozzo. In a very short time, because of his skill and his boldness of body and mind, he became the first man of Vitellozzo's troops. However, since he felt it was demeaning to serve under others, he decided, with Vitellozzo's help and with the assistance of some of its citizens (those who preferred servitude to the liberty of their native city), to take over Fermo. He wrote to Giovanni Fogliani that, since he had been away from home for so long, he wanted both to come to see him and his city and to check his inheritance. Since he had exerted himself for no other reason than to acquire honour, he wanted to arrive in honourable fashion, accompanied by an escort of a hundred horsemen from among his friends and servants, so that his fellow citizens might see that he had not spent his time in vain. In addition, he begged his uncle to arrange for an honourable reception from the people of Fermo, one that might bring honour not only to Giovanni but also to himself as his pupil.

Therefore, Giovanni in no way failed in his duty toward his nephew: he had him received in honourable fashion by the people of Fermo, and he gave him rooms in his own dwellings. After a few days had passed and he had secretly made the preparations necessary for his forthcoming wickedness, Oliverotto gave a magnificent solemn banquet,* to which he invited Giovanni

Fogliani and all of the first citizens of Fermo. When the meal and all the other entertainments customary at such banquets were completed, Oliverotto artfully began to discuss serious matters, speaking of the greatness of Pope Alexander and his son Cesare, and of their undertakings. After Giovanni and the others had replied to his arguments, he suddenly arose, declaring that these were matters to be discussed in a more secluded place, and withdrew into another room. Giovanni and all the other citizens followed him. No sooner were they seated than, from secret places in the room, soldiers emerged who killed Giovanni and all the others.* After this murder Oliverotto mounted his horse, paraded through the town, and besieged the chief officials in the government palace. They were forced to obey him out of fear, and to constitute a government of which he made himself prince. After he killed all those who might have harmed him because they were unhappy with the situation, he strengthened his power by instituting new civil and military institutions. As a result, in the space of the year that he held the principality, not only was he secure in the city of Fermo, but he had become feared by all its neighbours. His expulsion would have been as difficult as that of Agathocles, if he had not let himself be tricked by Cesare Borgia (as was noted above), when the Duke captured the Orsini and the Vitelli at Senigallia. There Oliverotto too was captured, a year after he committed his parricide,* and together with Vittellozzo, who had been his teacher in his virtues and wickedness, he was strangled.

One might well wonder how, after so many betrayals and cruelties, Agathocles and others like him could live for such a long time secure in their native cities and defend themselves from foreign enemies without being plotted against by their own citizens. Many others, employing cruel means, were unable to hold on to their state even in peaceful times, not to speak of the uncertain times of war. I believe that this depends on whether cruelty be badly or well used.* Those cruelties are well used (if it is permitted to speak well of evil) that are carried out in a single stroke, done out of necessity to protect oneself, and then are not continued, but are instead converted into the greatest possible benefits for the subjects. Those cruelties are badly used that, although few at the outset, increase with the passing of time instead of disappearing. Those who follow the first method can remedy their standing, both with God and with men, as Agathocles did; the others cannot possibly maintain their positions.

Hence it should be noted that, in conquering a state, its conqueror should weigh all the injurious things he must do and commit them all at once, so as not to have to repeat them every day. By not repeating them, he will be able to make men feel secure and win them over with the benefits he bestows upon them. Anyone who does otherwise, either out of timidity or because of bad advice, is always obliged to keep his knife in his hand. Nor can he ever count upon his subjects, who, because of their recent and continuous injuries, cannot feel secure with him. Therefore, injuries should be inflicted all at once, for the less they are tasted, the less harm they do. However, benefits should be distributed a little at a time, so that they may be fully savoured. Above all, a prince should live with his subjects in such a way that no unforeseen event, either bad or good, may cause him to alter his course; for when difficulties arise in adverse conditions, you do not have time to resort to cruelty, and the good that you do will help you very little, since it will be judged a forced measure, and you will earn from it no gratitude whatsoever.

IX
Of the civil principality
[*De principatu civili*]

BUT let us come to the second instance, when a private citizen becomes prince of his native city not through wickedness or any other intolerable violence, but with the favour of his fellow citizens. This can be called a civil principality, the acquisition of which neither depends completely upon virtue nor upon Fortune, but instead upon a fortunate astuteness. I maintain that

one reaches this princedom either with the favour of the com
people or with that of the nobility, since these two different
humours* are found in every body politic. They arise from the
fact that the people do not wish to be commanded or oppressed
by the nobles, while the nobles do desire to command and to
oppress the people. From these two opposed appetites, there
arises in cities one of three effects: a principality, liberty, or
licence. A principality is brought about either by the common
people or by the nobility, depending on which of the two parties
has the opportunity. When the nobles see that they cannot resist
the populace, they begin to support someone from among themselves, and make him prince in order to be able to satisfy their
appetites under his protection. The common people as well, seeing that they cannot resist the nobility, give their support to one
man so as to be defended by his authority. He who attains the
principality with the help of the nobility maintains it with more
difficulty than he who becomes prince with the help of the
common people, for he finds himself a prince amidst many who
feel themselves to be his equals, and because of this he can
neither govern nor manage them as he wishes. But he who
attains the principality through popular favour finds himself
alone, and has around him either no one or very few who are not
ready to obey him. Besides this, one cannot honestly satisfy the
nobles without harming others, but the common people can certainly be satisfied. Their desire is more just than that of the
nobles—the former want not to be oppressed, while the latter
want to oppress. In addition, a prince can never make himself
secure when the people are his enemy, because there are so many
of them; he can make himself secure against the nobles, because
they are so few. The worst that a prince can expect from a
hostile people is to be abandoned by them; but with a hostile
nobility, not only does he have to fear being abandoned, but also
that they will oppose him. Since the nobles are more perceptive
and cunning, they always have time to save themselves, seeking
the favours of the side they believe will prevail. Furthermore, a
prince must always live with the same common people, but he
can easily do without the same nobles, having the power every

day to make and unmake them, or to take away and restore their power as he sees fit.

In order better to clarify this point, let me say that the nobles should be considered chiefly in two ways: either they conduct themselves in such a way that they commit themselves completely to your cause, or they do not. Those who commit themselves and are not rapacious should be honoured and loved. Those who do not commit themselves can be evaluated in two ways. If they act in this manner out of pusillanimity and a natural lack of courage, you should make use of them, especially those who are wise advisers, since in prosperous times they will gain you honour, and in adverse times you need not fear them. But when, cunningly and influenced by ambition, they refrain from committing themselves to you, this is a sign that they think more of themselves than of you. The prince should be on guard against them and fear them as if they were declared enemies, because they will always help to bring about his downfall in adverse times.

Therefore, one who becomes prince with the support of the common people must keep them well disposed. This is easy for him, since the only thing they ask of him is not to be oppressed. But one who becomes prince with the help of the nobility against the will of the common people must, before all else, seek to win the people's support, which should be easy if he takes them under his protection. Because men who are well treated by those from whom they expected harm are more obliged to their benefactor, the common people quickly become better disposed toward him than if he had become prince with their support. A prince can gain their favour in various ways, but because these vary according to the situation, no fixed rules can be given for them, and therefore I shall not discuss them. I shall conclude by saying only that a prince must have the friendship of the common people. Otherwise, he will have no support in times of adversity. Nabis, Prince of the Spartans, withstood a siege by all of Greece and by one of Rome's most victorious armies, and he defended his native city and his own state against them. When danger suddenly approached, he needed only to protect himself from a few of his subjects, but if he had had the common people hostile, this would not have been sufficient.

Let no one contradict my opinion by citing that trite proverb, claiming he who builds upon the people builds upon mud; for that is true when a private citizen makes them his foundation, and allows himself to believe that the common people will free him if he is oppressed by enemies or by the public officials. In such a case, a man might often find himself deceived, as were the Gracchi in Rome or as Messer Giorgio Scali was in Florence. When the prince who builds his foundations on the people is a man able to command and of spirit, is not bewildered by adversities, does not fail to make other preparations, and is a leader who keeps up the spirits of the populace through his courage and his institutions, he will never find himself deceived by the common people, and he will discover that he has laid his foundations well.

Principalities of this type are usually endangered when they are about to change from a civil government into an absolute form of government. For these princes rule either by themselves or by means of public magistrates. In the latter case, their status is weaker and more dangerous, since they depend entirely upon the will of those citizens who are appointed as magistrates. These men can very easily (especially in adverse times) seize the state, either by abandoning him or by opposing him. And in such periods of danger the prince has no time for seizing absolute authority, since the citizens and subjects* who are used to receiving their orders from the magistrates are not willing to obey his orders in these crises. And in doubtful times he will always find a scarcity of men in whom he can trust. Such a prince cannot rely upon what he sees during periods of calm when the citizens need his rule, because then everyone comes running, everyone makes promises, and each person is willing to die for him, since death is remote. But in times of adversity, when the state needs its citizens, then few are to be found. And this experiment is all the more dangerous since it can be tried but once. Therefore, a wise prince must think of a method by which his citizens will need the state and himself at all times and in every circumstance. Then they will always be loyal to him.

X

How the strength of all principalities should be measured

[Quomodo omnium principatuum vires perpendi debeant]

IN examining the qualities of these principalities, another consideration arises: that is, whether the prince has so much power that he can (if necessary) stand up on his own, or whether he always needs the protection of others. In order to clarify this matter, let me say that I judge those princes self-sufficient who, either through abundance of troops or of money, are capable of gathering together a suitable army and of fighting a battle against whoever might attack them. I consider men who always need the protection of others to be those who cannot meet their enemy in the field, but must seek refuge behind their city walls and defend them. The first case has already been treated,* and later on I shall say whatever else is necessary on the subject. Nothing more can be added to the second case than to encourage such princes to fortify and provision their own cities, and not to concern themselves with the surrounding countryside. Anyone who has fortified his city well, and has managed his affairs well with his subjects in the manner I discussed above and discuss below, will be attacked only with great hesitation, for men are always enemies of undertakings in which they foresee difficulties, and it cannot seem easy to attack someone whose city is well fortified and who is not hated by his people.

The cities of Germany are completely independent, they control little surrounding territory, they obey the emperor when they please, and they fear neither him nor any other nearby power. For they are fortified in such a manner that everyone considers their capture to be a tedious and difficult affair. They all have appropriate moats and walls; they have enough artillery; they always store in their public warehouses enough drink, food, and fuel for a year. Besides all this, in order to be able to keep the lower classes fed without loss of public funds, they always keep in reserve a year's supply of raw materials sufficient to give these people work at those trades that are the nerves and lifeblood of that city and of the industries from which the people earn their living. Moreover, they hold the military arts in high regard, and they have many regulations for maintaining them.

Therefore, a prince who has a city organized in this fashion and who does not make himself hated cannot be attacked. Even if he were to be attacked, the enemy would have to retreat in shame, for the affairs of this world are so changeable that it is almost impossible for anyone to sustain a siege for a year with his troops idle. And if it is objected that when the people have their possessions outside the city, and see them destroyed, they will lose patience, and that the long siege and self-interest will cause them to forget their love for their prince, let me reply that a prudent and spirited prince will always overcome all such difficulties, inspiring his subjects now with hope that the evil will not last long, now with fear of the enemy's cruelty, now by protecting himself with clever manoeuvres against those who seem too outspoken. Besides this, the enemy will in all likelihood burn and lay waste to the surrounding country upon their arrival, just when the spirits of the defenders are still ardent and determined on the city's defence. And thus the prince has so much the less to fear, because after a few days, when their spirits have cooled down somewhat, the damage has already been inflicted and the evils suffered, and there is no longer any remedy for them. Now the people will rally around their prince even more, for it would appear that he is bound to them by obligations, since their homes were burned and their possessions destroyed in his defence. The nature of men is such that they find themselves obligated as much for the benefits they confer as for those they receive. Thus, if everything is taken into consideration, it will not be difficult for a prudent prince to keep the spirits of his citizens firm during the siege before and after this destruction, so long as he does not lack sufficient food and weapons for his defence.

XI

Of ecclesiastical principalities
[*De principatibus ecclesiasticis*]

ONLY ecclesiastical principalities now remain to be discussed. Concerning these, all the problems occur before they are acquired, since they are acquired either through virtue or through Fortune, and are maintained without one or the other. They are sustained by the ancient institutions of religion, which are so powerful and of such a quality that they keep their princes in power no matter how they act and live their lives. These princes alone have states and do not defend them; have subjects and do not govern them; and their states, though undefended, are never taken away from them; and their subjects, being ungoverned, show no concern, and do not think about severing their ties with them, nor are they able to. These principalities, then, are the only secure and successful ones. However, since they are protected by higher causes, that the human mind is unable to fathom, I shall not discuss them: being exalted and maintained by God, it would be the act of a presumptuous and foolhardy man to do so.* Nevertheless, someone might ask me why it is that the Church, in temporal matters, has arrived at such power when, until the time of Alexander, the Italian powers—not just those who were the established rulers, but every baron and lord, no matter how weak—considered her temporal power as insignificant, and now a King of France trembles before it, and it has been able to throw him out of Italy and to ruin the Venetians. Although this situation may already be known, it does not seem superfluous to me to recall it in some detail.

Before Charles, King of France, invaded Italy, this province was under the power of the Pope, the Venetians, the King of Naples, the Duke of Milan, and the Florentines. These rulers had two major concerns: first, that a foreigner might enter Italy with his armies; second, that no one of them should seize more territory.* Those whom they needed to watch most closely were the Pope and the Venetians. To restrain the Venetians, the alliance of all the rest was necessary, as was the case in the defence of Ferrara.* To keep the Pope in check, they made use of the Roman barons, who—divided into two factions (the Orsini and the Colonna)—always had a reason for squabbling amongst themselves. They kept the papacy weak and unstable, standing with their weapons in hand right under the eyes of the Pope. And although from time to time there arose a courageous pope like Pope Sixtus,* neither Fortune nor his wisdom could ever free him from these difficulties. The brevity of the reigns of the popes was the cause. In ten years (their average life expectancy), a pope might put down one of the factions with difficulty. If, for example, one pope almost wiped out the Colonna, a new pope who was the enemy of the Orsini would emerge, enabling the Colonna to grow powerful again, and yet he would not have sufficient time to destroy the Orsini. As a consequence, the temporal powers of the Pope were little respected in Italy.

Then Alexander VI came to power, and he, more than any of the popes who ever reigned, demonstrated how well a pope could succeed with money and his own troops. With Duke Valentino as his instrument and the French invasion as his opportunity, he achieved all those things that I discussed earlier in describing the actions of the Duke. And although his intention was to make the Duke and not the Church great, nevertheless, what he did resulted in the increase of the power of the Church, which after his death, and once the Duke was ruined, became the heir to his labours.

Then came Pope Julius, and he found the Church powerful, possessing all of the Romagna, having destroyed the Roman barons, and having annihilated their factions by Alexander's blows. He also found the way open for the accumulation of wealth by a method never before used by Alexander or his predecessors.* These practices Julius not only continued but also increased, and he planned to capture Bologna, to wipe out the Venetians, and to drive the French out of Italy. He succeeded in all these undertakings, and he is worthy of even more praise, since he did everything in order to increase the power of the Church, and not for any private individual. He also managed to keep the Orsini and the Colonna factions in the same condition in which he found them. Although there were some leaders among them who wanted to make changes, there were two things which held them back: first, the power of the Church, which frightened them; and second, not having any of their own family as cardinals, for these men were the source of the conflicts among them. These factions will never be at peace as long as they have cardinals, since such men foster factions (both in Rome and outside the city), and those barons are compelled to defend them. And thus, from the ambitions of the priests are born the disorders and the quarrels among the barons.

Therefore, His Holiness Pope Leo* has found the papacy extremely powerful. It is to be hoped that, if his predecessors made it great by feats of arms, he will make it extremely great and venerable through his natural goodness and his countless virtues.*

XII

Of the various kinds of troops and mercenary soldiers

[Quot sunt genera militiae et de mercenaries militibus]

HAVING treated in detail all the characteristics of those principalities that I proposed to discuss at the beginning, and having considered, to some extent, the reasons for their success or failure, and having demonstrated the methods by which many have tried to acquire them and to maintain them, it remains for me now to speak in general terms of the kinds of offence and defence that can be adopted by each of the previously mentioned principalities.

We have said above that a prince must have laid firm foundations; otherwise he will necessarily come to ruin. And the principal foundations of all states, the new as well as the old or the mixed, are good laws and good armies. Since good laws cannot exist where there are no good armies, and where good armies exist there must be good laws, I shall leave aside the arguments about laws and shall discuss the armed forces.

I say, then, that the armies with which a prince defends his state are made up of his own troops, or mercenaries, or auxiliaries, or of mixed troops. Mercenaries and auxiliaries are useless and dangerous. If a prince holds on to his state by means of mercenary armies, he will never be stable or secure. Mercenaries are disunited, ambitious, undisciplined, and disloyal. They are brave with their friends; with their enemies, they are cowards. They have no fear of God, and they keep no faith with men. Their ruin is deferred only so long as an attack is deferred. In peacetime you are plundered by them, in war by your enemies. The reason for this is that they have no other love nor other motive to keep them in the field than a meagre salary, which is not enough to make them want to die for you. They love being your soldiers when you are not waging war, but when war comes, they either flee or desert. This would require little effort to demonstrate, since the present ruin of Italy is caused by nothing other than its having relied on mercenary troops for a period of many years. These forces did, on occasion, help some to get ahead, and they appeared courageous in combat with other mercenaries. But when the invasion of the foreigner came,* they showed themselves for what they were, and thus Charles, King of France, was permitted to take Italy with a piece of chalk.* The man who said that our sins were the cause of this disaster spoke the truth;* but they were not at all those sins he had in mind, but rather these I have recounted; and because they were the sins of princes, the princes in turn have suffered the punishment for them.

I wish to demonstrate more fully the failure of such armies. Mercenary captains are either excellent men or they are not. If they are, you cannot trust them, since they will always aspire to their own greatness, either by oppressing you, who are their masters, or by oppressing others against your intent; but if the captain is without ability, he usually ruins you. If someone were to reply that anyone who bears arms will act in this manner, mercenary or not, I would answer that armies have to be commanded either by a prince or by a republic. The prince must go in person and perform the office of captain himself. A republic must send its own citizens, and when it sends one who does not turn out to be an able man, it must replace him. If he is capable, the republic must restrain him with laws so that he does not exceed his authority. We see from experience that only princes and republics armed with their own troops make very great progress, and that mercenaries cause nothing but damage. A republic armed with its own citizens is less likely to come under the rule of one of its citizens than a city armed with foreign soldiers.

Rome and Sparta for many centuries stood armed and free. The Swiss are extremely well armed and are very free. An example from antiquity of the use of mercenary troops is the Carthaginians. They were almost overcome by their own mercenary soldiers after the first war with the Romans, even though the Carthaginians had their own citizens as officers. Philip of Macedon was made captain of their army by the Thebans after the death of Epaminondas, and after the victory he took their liberty away from them. After the death of Duke Filippo, the Milanese employed Francesco Sforza to wage war against the Venetians; having defeated the enemy at Caravaggio,* he joined with them to oppress the Milanese, his employers. Sforza, his father,* being in the employ of Queen Giovanna of Naples, all at once left her without defences. Because of this, so as not to lose her kingdom, she was forced to throw herself into the lap of the King of Aragon. And if the Venetians and the Florentines have in the past increased their dominion with such soldiers, and their captains have not yet made themselves princes but have, instead, defended them, I answer that the Florentines have been favoured in this matter by luck. Among their able captains whom they could have had reason to fear, some did not win, others met with opposition, and others turned their ambition elsewhere. The one who did not win was John Hawkwood, whose loyalty will never be known since he did not win. But anyone will admit that, had he succeeded, the Florentines would have been at his mercy. Sforza always had Braccio's soldiers as enemies, so that each checked the other. Francesco turned his ambition to Lombardy, Braccio against the Church and the Kingdom of Naples.

But let us come to what has occurred just recently. The Florentines made Paulo Vitelli their captain, a very able man and one who rose from being a private citizen to achieve great prestige. If he had captured Pisa, no one would deny that the Florentines would have had to become his ally. If he had become employed by their enemies, they would have had no defence, and if they had kept him on, they would have been obliged to obey him. As for the Venetians, if we examine the course they followed, we see that they operated securely and gloriously as long as they fought with their own troops (this was before they began to fight on the mainland); with their nobles and their common people armed, they fought courageously [at sea]. But when they began to fight on land, they abandoned this successful strategy and followed the usual practices of waging war in Italy. As they first began to expand their territory on the mainland, since they did not have much to control there and enjoyed great prestige, they had little to fear from their captains. When their territory increased, which happened under Carmagnola, the Venetians had a taste of this mistake. Having found him very able (since under his command they had defeated the Duke of Milan), and knowing, on the other hand, that he had cooled off in waging war, they judged that they could no longer conquer under him, for he had no wish to do so. Yet they could not dismiss him, for fear of losing what they had acquired. So, in order to secure themselves against him, they were forced to execute him. Then they had as their captains Bartolomeo da Bergamo, Roberto da San Severino, the Count of Pitigliano, and the like. With men such as these they had to fear their losses, not their acquisitions, as occurred later at Vailà,* where, in a single day,* they lost what had cost them eight hundred years of exhausting effort to acquire.* From these kinds of soldiers, therefore, come only slow, tardy, and weak conquests but sudden and astonishing losses.

And since with these examples I have begun to treat of Italy, which for many years has been ruled by mercenary soldiers, I should like to discuss them in greater depth, so that once their origins and developments are uncovered they can be more easily corrected. You must, then, understand how in recent times, when the Empire began to be driven out of Italy and the Pope began to win more prestige in temporal affairs, Italy was divided into many states. Many of the large cities took up arms against their nobles, who (at first backed by the Emperor) had kept them under their control. The Church supported these cities to increase its temporal power; in many other cities, citizens became princes. Hence, after Italy came almost entirely into the hands of the Church and of several republics, those priests and other citizens who were not accustomed to bearing arms began to hire foreigners. The first to give prestige to such troops was Alberigo of Conio from the Romagna. From this man's training emerged, among others, Braccio and Sforza, who in their day were the arbiters of Italy. After them came all the others who have commanded these soldiers until the present day. The result of their skills has been that Italy has been overrun by Charles, plundered by Louis, violated by Ferdinand, and insulted by the Swiss.

Their method was, first, to increase the prestige of their own soldiers by taking away the prestige of the infantry. They did so because they were men without a state of their own, who lived by their profession; a small number of foot-soldiers could not give them prestige, and they could not afford to hire a large number of them. So they relied completely upon cavalry, since for possessing only a reasonable number of horsemen they were provided for and honoured. They reduced matters to such a state that in an army of twenty thousand troops, one could hardly find two thousand foot-soldiers. Besides this, they had used every means to spare themselves and their soldiers fear and hardship, not killing each other in their scuffles, but instead taking each other prisoner without demanding ransom. They would not attack cities at night. Those in the cities would not attack the tents of the besiegers. They built neither stockades nor trenches around their camps. They did not campaign in the winter. And all these things were permitted by their military institutions and gave them a means of escaping hardships and dangers, as was mentioned. As a result, these *condottieri* have conducted Italy into slavery and disgrace.*

XIII

Of auxiliary, mixed, and citizen soldiers
[*De militibus auxiliariis, mixtis et propriis*]

THE other kind of worthless army, auxiliary troops, are those that arrive when you call a powerful prince to bring his forces to your aid and defence, as was done in recent times by Pope Julius, who, having witnessed the sad showing of his mercenary soldiers in the campaign of Ferrara, turned to auxiliary soldiers and made an agreement with Ferdinand, King of Spain, that he should assist him with his soldiers and his armies.* These soldiers can be useful and good in themselves, but for the man who summons them they are almost always harmful. If they lose, you are destroyed; if they win, you end up their prisoner. And although ancient histories are full of such examples, nevertheless I do not wish to leave unexamined this recent example of Pope Julius, whose policy could not have been more poorly considered; for he threw himself completely into the hands of a foreigner in his desire to take Ferrara. But his good luck caused a third development, so that he did not reap the fruits of his ill-advised decision. After his auxiliaries were routed at Ravenna,* the Swiss rose up and chased out the victors, to the surprise of Pope Julius as well as everyone else. Thus, he was neither taken prisoner by his enemies, who had fled, nor by his auxiliaries, since he triumphed with troops other than theirs. Completely unarmed, the Florentines engaged ten thousand French soldiers to take Pisa:* such a plan endangered them more than any of their previous predicaments. In order to oppose his neighbours, the Emperor of Constantinople* brought ten thousand Turkish troops into Greece: when the war was over they did not want to leave, and this was the beginning of Greek servitude under the infidel.

Anyone, therefore, who wishes to be unable to win should make use of these soldiers, for they are much more dangerous than mercenary troops. With them ruin is assured, for they are completely united and completely under the command of others. Whereas, after they have been victorious mercenaries require more time and a better opportunity if they are to injure you, for they are not a single body of men and they have been brought together and paid by you. Any third party whom you might make their commander cannot immediately seize enough authority to harm you. In short, with mercenaries the greatest danger is their reluctance to fight; with auxiliaries, their military virtue. A wise prince has always avoided these soldiers and has turned to his own troops. He has preferred to lose with his own troops rather than to win with those of others, judging that to be no true victory which has been gained by means of foreign troops.

I shall never hesitate to cite Cesare Borgia and his actions. This Duke entered the Romagna with auxiliary troops, leading an army composed entirely of Frenchmen; and with them he captured Imola and Forlì.* But not considering such troops reliable, he turned to mercenary forces, judging them to be less dangerous, and he hired the Orsini and the Vitelli. When he found, in managing them, that they were unreliable, disloyal, and dangerous, he got rid of them and turned to his own men. And it is easy to see the difference between these two sorts of troops, if we consider the difference between the Duke's reputation when he had only French troops or when he had the Orsini and the Vitelli, as opposed to when he was left with his own troops and depending on himself. We find that his prestige always grew. Never was he esteemed more highly than when everyone saw that he was completely in command of his own troops.

I did not wish to depart from citing recent Italian examples, yet I do not want to omit Hiero of Syracuse, one of those I mentioned above. This man, as I said, having been named by the Syracusans commander of their armies, immediately realized that mercenary forces were useless, since their *condottieri* were men like our Italian *condottieri*. It seemed to him that he could neither keep them on nor dismiss them, so he had them all cut to pieces. Afterwards he waged war with his own troops, and not with those belonging to others.

I should also like to call to mind a figure from the Old Testament* that suits this topic. David offered himself to Saul to fight Goliath, the Philistine challenger. In order to give him courage, Saul armed him with his own armour, which David cast off after putting it on, declaring that with it he could not test his true worth. He therefore wished to meet the enemy with his own sling and his own knife. In short, the weapons of others slide off your back, weigh you down, or tie you up.

Having freed France from the English* by means of his Fortune and his virtue, Charles VII, father of King Louis XI, recognized the necessity of arming himself with his own men, and he set up an ordinance to procure cavalry and infantry in his kingdom.* Later, his son King Louis abolished the ordinance of the infantry and began to hire Swiss troops.* This error, followed by others, as we can now observe from events, is the cause of the threats to that kingdom. By giving prestige to the Swiss, he discredited his own troops, for he did away entirely with his footsoldiers and obliged his cavalry to depend upon the abilities of others. Being accustomed to fighting with the aid of the Swiss, the French cavalry felt they could not win without them. From this, it came about that the French were not strong enough to match the Swiss, and without the Swiss they did not test their chances. The armies of France, therefore, have been mixed, partly mercenaries and partly her own troops. Armies combined together in such a fashion are much better than a purely auxiliary force or a purely mercenary army, but are greatly inferior to one's own troops. And the example just cited should suffice, for the Kingdom of France would be invincible if Charles's military institutions had been developed or preserved. But the poor judgement of men will begin something that seems good at the outset without noticing the poison concealed underneath, as I said earlier in connection with consumptive fevers. And thus anyone who does not diagnose the ills when they arise in a principality is not really wise, and this talent is given to few men. If one looks for the first signs of the downfall of the Roman Empire it will be found to have begun with the hiring of the Goths as mercenaries.* From that beginning the armed forces of the

Roman Empire began to be weakened, and all the virtue taken away from it was given over to the Goths.

I conclude, therefore, that without having one's own soldiers, no principality is safe. On the contrary, it is completely subject to Fortune, not having the virtue that defends it faithfully in adverse times. It was always the opinion and conviction of wise men, 'quod nihil sit tam infirmum aut instabile quam fama potentie non sua vi nixa'* ['that nothing is so unhealthy or unstable as the reputation for power that is not based upon one's own forces']. One's own soldiers are those composed either of subjects or of citizens or your own dependants; all others are either mercenaries or auxiliaries. The means of ordering one's own arms are easily discovered, if the methods followed by those four men* I have cited above are examined, and if one observes how Philip, father of Alexander the Great,* and many republics and princes have armed and organized themselves. I take my stand entirely on such methods.

XIV

A prince's duty concerning military matters

[*Quod principem deceat circa militiam*]

A PRINCE, therefore, must not have any other object nor any other thought, nor must he adopt anything as his art but war, its institutions, and its discipline; because that is the only art* befitting one who commands. This discipline is of such efficacy that not only does it maintain those who were born princes, but it enables men of private station on many occasions to rise to that position. On the other hand, it is evident that when princes have given more thought to delicate refinements than to military concerns, they have lost their state. The most important reason why you lose it is by neglecting this art, while the way to acquire it is to be well versed in this art.

Francesco Sforza became Duke of Milan from being a private citizen because he was armed. Since his sons* avoided the hardships of military service, they became private citizens after having been dukes. Among the other bad effects it brings with it, being unarmed makes you contemptible. This is one of those infamies a prince should be on guard against, as will be discussed below. Between an armed and an unarmed man there is no comparison whatsoever, and it is not reasonable for an armed man to obey an unarmed man willingly, nor for an unarmed man to be safe among armed servants: when the one is full of scorn and the other is suspicious, it is impossible for them to work well together. Therefore, as was said, a prince who does not understand military matters, besides other misfortunes, cannot be esteemed by his own soldiers, nor can he trust them.

He should, therefore, never take his mind from this exercise of war, and in peacetime he must train himself more than in time of war. This can be done in two ways: first, through physical exercise; second, by study. As far as physical exercise is concerned, besides keeping his men well ordered and exercised, he must always be out hunting and must accustom his body to hardships in this way; and he must also learn the nature of terrains, and know how mountains rise, how valleys open, how plains lie, and understand the nature of rivers and swamps; and he should devote a great deal of attention to such activities. Such knowledge is useful in two ways: first, one learns to know one's own country and can better understand how to defend it; second, with the knowledge and experience of these terrains, one can easily comprehend the characteristics of any other site that it is necessary to explore for the first time. The hills, valleys, plains, rivers, and swamps of Tuscany, for example, have certain similarities to those of other territories, so that by knowing the lie of the land in one territory, one can easily come to know it in others. A prince who lacks this expertise lacks the most important quality in a commander, because it teaches you to find the enemy, choose a campsite, lead troops, organize them for battles, and besiege towns to your own advantage.

Among other praises bestowed upon him by writers, Philopoemen, Prince of the Achaeans, is praised because in peacetime he thought of nothing except the ways of waging war. When he was out in the country with his friends, he often stopped and reasoned with them: 'If the enemy were on that hilltop and we were here with our army, which of the two of us would have the advantage? How could we attack them without breaking formation? If we wanted to retreat, how could we do this? If they were to retreat, how could we pursue them?' As they rode along, he proposed to them every situation in which an army might find itself; he heard their opinions, expressed his own, and backed it up with reasons.* As a result, because of these continuous reflections no unforeseen incident could arise when he was leading his troops, for which he did not have the remedy.

But as for study, the prince must read histories and in them consider the deeds of excellent men. He must see how they conducted themselves in wars. He must examine the reasons for their victories and for their defeats, in order to avoid the latter and to imitate the former. Above all else, he must do as some eminent men before him have done, who elected to imitate someone who had been praised and honoured before them, and always keep in mind his deeds and actions: just as it is reported that Alexander the Great imitated Achilles, Caesar imitated Alexander, and Scipio imitated Cyrus.* Anyone who reads the life of Cyrus written by Xenophon* will realize how important in the life of Scipio such imitation was for his glory and how closely in purity,* goodness, humanity, and generosity Scipio conformed to those characteristics of Cyrus about which Xenophon had written.

A wise prince must follow such methods as these and never be idle in peaceful times, but he must turn them diligently to his advantage in order to be able to profit from them in times of adversity, so that when Fortune changes she will find him prepared to resist her.

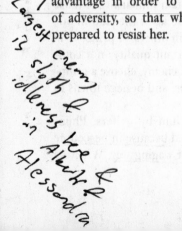

Laziest enemy
is sloth &
idleness here
in Alberti &
Alessandra

XV

Of those things for which men, and particularly princes, are praised or blamed

[De his rebus quibus homines et presertim principes laudantur aut vituperantur]

NOW, it remains to be considered what should be the methods and principles of a prince in dealing with his subjects and allies. Because I know that many have written about this,* I am afraid that by writing about it again I shall be considered presumptuous, especially since in discussing this material I depart from the procedures of others. But since my intention is to write something useful for anyone who understands it, it seemed more suitable for me to search after the effectual truth of the matter rather than its imagined one. Many writers have imagined republics and principalities that have never been seen nor known to exist in reality. For there is such a distance between how one lives and how one ought to live, that anyone who abandons what is done for what ought to be done achieves his downfall rather than his preservation. A man who wishes to profess goodness at all times will come to ruin among so many who are not good. Therefore, it is necessary for a prince who wishes to maintain himself to learn how not to be good, and to use this knowledge or not to use it according to necessity.

Leaving aside, therefore, matters concerning an imaginary prince, and taking into account those that are true, let me say that all men, when they are spoken of—and especially princes, since they are placed on a higher level—are judged by some of those qualities that bring them either blame or praise. And this is why one is considered generous, another miserly (to use a Tuscan word, since 'avaricious' in our language is still used to mean one who wishes to acquire by means of theft; we call 'miserly' one who is excessive in avoiding using what he has). One is considered a giver, the other rapacious; one cruel, the other merciful;

one a breaker of faith, the other faithful; one effeminate and cowardly, the other fierce and courageous; one humane, the other proud; one lascivious, the other chaste; one trustworthy, the other shrewd; one hard, the other easygoing; one serious, the other frivolous; one religious, the other unbelieving; and the like. And I know that everyone will admit it would be a very praiseworthy thing to find in a prince those qualities mentioned above that are held to be good. But since it is neither possible to have them nor to observe them all completely, because the human condition does not permit it, a prince must be prudent enough to know how to escape the infamy of those vices that would take the state away from him, and be on guard against those vices that will not take it from him, whenever possible. But if he cannot, he need not concern himself unduly if he ignores these less serious vices. Moreover, he need not worry about incurring the infamy of those vices without which it would be difficult to save the state. Because, carefully taking everything into account, he will discover that something which appears to be a virtue,* if pursued, will result in his ruin; while some other thing which seems to be a vice, if pursued, will secure his safety and his well-being.

XVI
Of generosity and miserliness
[*De liberalitate et parsimonia*]

BEGINNING, therefore, with the first of the above-mentioned qualities, I say that it would be good to be considered generous. Nevertheless, generosity employed in such a way as to give you a reputation for it will injure you, because if it is employed virtuously* and as one should employ it, it will not be recognized, and you will not avoid the infamy of its opposite. And so, if a prince wants to maintain his reputation for generosity among men, it is necessary for him not to neglect any possible means of sumptuous display; in so doing, such a prince will always use up all his resources in such displays, and will eventually be obliged, if he wishes to maintain his reputation for generosity, to burden the people with excessive taxes and to do all those things one does to procure money. This will begin to make him hateful to his subjects and, if he becomes impoverished, he will be held in low regard by everyone. As a consequence of this generosity of his, having injured the many and rewarded the few, he will feel the effects of any discontent and will vacillate at the first sign of danger; recognizing this and wishing to change his ways, he immediately incurs the infamy of being a miser. Therefore, a prince, being unable to use this virtue of generosity in a manner that will not harm himself if he is known for it, should, if he is wise, not concern himself about the reputation of being miserly. With time he will come to be considered more generous, once it is evident that, as a result of his parsimony, his income is sufficient, he can defend himself from anyone who wages war against him, and he can undertake enterprises without overburdening his people. In this way he appears as generous to all those from whom he takes nothing, who are countless, and as miserly to all those to whom he gives nothing, who are few.

In our times we have not seen great deeds accomplished except by those who were considered miserly; the others were all wiped out. Although he made use of his reputation for generosity in order to gain the papacy,* Pope Julius II then decided not to maintain this reputation, in order to be able to wage war. The present King of France* has waged many wars without imposing extraordinary taxes on his subjects, only because his habitual parsimony has provided for the additional expenditures. If he had been considered generous, the present King of Spain* would not have engaged in or successfully carried out so many enterprises. Therefore—in order not to have to rob his subjects, to be able to defend himself, not to become poor and contemptible, and not to be forced to become rapacious—a prince must consider it of little account if he incurs the reputation of being a miser, for this is one of those vices that enables him to rule. And if someone were to say: 'Caesar with his generosity achieved imperial power, and many others, because they were generous and known to be so, achieved very high positions', I would reply: You are either already a prince, or you are on the way to becoming one. In the first case such generosity is damaging; in the second, it is indeed necessary to be thought generous. Caesar was one of those who wanted to gain the principality of Rome; but if he had survived and had not moderated his expenditures after doing so, he would have destroyed the power he acquired.* And if someone were to reply: 'There have existed many princes who have accomplished great deeds with their armies who have been considered generous', I would answer you: A prince either spends his own money and that of his subjects, or that of others. In the first case he must be economical; in the second, he must not hold back any part of his generosity. For the prince who goes out with his armies and lives by looting, sacking, and ransoms, and who lays hands on the property of others, such generosity is necessary; otherwise he would not be followed by his soldiers. Of what is not yours or your subjects, you can be a more generous donor, as were Cyrus, Caesar, and Alexander: spending the wealth of others does not lessen your reputation, but only adds to it. Only the spending of your own is what does you harm. There is nothing that uses itself up faster than generosity; for as you employ it, you lose the means of employing it, and you become either poor or despised or else, to escape poverty, you become rapacious and hated. And above all things, a prince must guard himself against being despised and hated. Generosity leads you both to one and to the other. So it is wiser to live with the reputation of a miser, which gives birth to an infamy without hatred, than to be forced to incur the reputation of rapacity because you want to be considered generous, which gives birth to an infamy with hatred.

XVII

Of cruelty and mercy, and whether it is better to be loved than to be feared or the contrary

[De crudelitate et pietate; et an sit melius amari quam timeri, vel e contra]

TURNING to the other qualities mentioned above, let me say that every prince must desire to be considered merciful and not cruel; nevertheless, he must take care not to use such mercy badly. Cesare Borgia was considered cruel; nonetheless, this cruelty of his brought order to the Romagna,* united it, and restored it to peace and loyalty. If we examine this carefully, we shall see that he was more merciful than the Florentine people, who allowed the destruction of Pistoia in order to avoid being considered cruel.* Therefore, a prince must not worry about the infamy of being considered cruel when it is a matter of keeping his subjects united and loyal. With a very few examples of cruelty, he will prove more compassionate than those who, out of excessive mercy, permit disorders to continue from which arise murders and plundering, for these usually injure the entire community, while the executions ordered by the prince injure specific individuals. Of all the types of princes, the new prince cannot escape the reputation for cruelty, since new states are full of dangers. Thus Virgil, through the mouth of Dido, declares: 'Res dura et regni novitas me talia cogunt moliri et late fines custode tueri'* ['The harshness of things and the newness of my rule make me act in such a manner, and to set guards over my land on all sides']. Nevertheless, a prince must be cautious in believing accusations and in acting against individuals, nor should he be afraid of his own shadow. He should proceed in such a manner, tempered by prudence and humanity, that too much trust may not render him incautious, nor too much suspicion render him insufferable.

From this arises an argument: whether it is better to be loved than to be feared, or the contrary. The answer is that one would like to be both one and the other. But since it is difficult to be both together, it is much safer to be feared than to be loved, when one of the two must be lacking. For one can generally say this about men: they are ungrateful, fickle, simulators and deceivers, avoiders of danger, and greedy for gain. While you work for their benefit they are completely yours, offering you their blood, their property, their lives, and their sons, as I said above, when the need to do so is far away. But when it draws nearer to you, they turn away. The prince who relies entirely upon their words comes to ruin, finding himself stripped naked of other preparations. For friendships acquired by a price and not by greatness and nobility of spirit are purchased but are not owned, and at the proper time cannot be spent. Men are less hesitant about injuring someone who makes himself loved than one who makes himself feared, because love is held together by a chain of obligation that, since men are a wretched lot, is broken on every occasion for their own self-interest; but fear is sustained by a dread of punishment that will never abandon you.

A prince must nevertheless make himself feared in such a way that he will avoid hatred, even if he does not acquire love; since one can very easily be feared and yet not hated. This will always be the case when he abstains from the property of his citizens and subjects, and from their women. If he must spill someone's blood, he should do this when there is proper justification and manifest cause. But above all else, he should abstain from seizing the property of others; for men forget the death of their father more quickly than the loss of their patrimony. Moreover, reasons for taking their property are never lacking, and he who begins to live by stealing always finds a reason for taking what belongs to others; reasons for spilling blood, on the other hand, are rarer and more fleeting.

But when the prince is with his armies and has a multitude of soldiers under his command, then it is absolutely necessary that he should not worry about being considered cruel, for without that reputation he will never keep an army united or prepared for any action. Numbered among the remarkable deeds of Hannibal is this: that while he had a very large army made up of all kinds of men that he commanded in foreign lands, there never arose the slightest dissension, either among themselves or against their leader, both during his periods of good and bad luck.* This could not have arisen from anything other than his inhuman cruelty, which, along with his many other virtues, made him always venerable and terrifying in the eyes of his soldiers. Without that quality, his other virtues would not have sufficed to attain the same effect. Having considered this matter very superficially, historians on the one hand admire these deeds of his, and on the other condemn the main cause of them.

That it is true that his other virtues would not have been sufficient can be seen from the case of Scipio, a most extraordinary man, not only in his time but in all of recorded history, whose armies in Spain rebelled against him. This came about from nothing other than his excessive compassion, which gave his soldiers more licence than is suitable to military discipline. For this he was censured in the Senate by Fabius Maximus, who called him the corruptor of the Roman army. When Locri was destroyed by one of his legates,* the Locrians were not avenged by him, nor was the arrogance of that legate corrected, all this arising from his easygoing nature. Someone in the Senate who tried to excuse him declared that there were many men who knew how not to err better than they knew how to correct their mistakes. In time such a character* would have damaged Scipio's fame and glory if he had long continued to command armies, but, living under the control of the Senate, this harmful quality of his was not only concealed but also contributed to his glory.

Let me conclude, then—returning to the issue of being feared and loved—that since men love at their own pleasure and fear at the pleasure of the prince, the wise prince should build his foundation upon that which is his own, not upon that which belongs to others: only he must seek to avoid being hated, as I have said.

XVIII

How a prince should keep his word

[*Quomodo fides a principibus sit servanda*]

How praiseworthy it is for a prince to keep his word and to live
with integrity and not by cunning, everyone knows. Nevertheless,
one sees from experience in our times that the princes who have
accomplished great deeds are those who have thought little about
keeping faith and who have known how cunningly to manipulate
men's minds; and in the end they have surpassed those who laid
their foundations upon sincerity.

Therefore, you must know that there are two modes of fighting: one in accordance with the laws, the other with force.* The
first is proper to man, the second to beasts. But because the first,
in many cases, is not sufficient, it becomes necessary to have
recourse to the second: therefore, a prince must know how to
make good use of the natures of both the beast and the man. This
rule was taught to princes symbolically by the writers of
antiquity: they recounted how Achilles and many others of those
ancient princes were given to Chiron the centaur to be raised and
cared for under his discipline. This can only mean* that, having a
half-beast and half-man as a teacher, a prince must know how to
employ the nature of the one and the other; for the one without
the other is not lasting.

Since, then, a prince must know how to make use of the nature
of the beast, he should choose from among the beasts the fox and
the lion;* for the lion cannot defend itself from traps, while the
fox cannot protect itself from the wolves. It is therefore necessary
to be a fox, in order to recognize the traps, and a lion, in order to
frighten the wolves: those who base their behaviour only on the
lion do not understand things. A wise ruler, therefore, cannot and
should not keep his word when such an observance would be to
his disadvantage, and when the reasons that caused him to make a
promise are removed. If men were all good, this precept would

[handwritten marginalia, left margin:] Surely it is self-interest or self-rule of man specify how thereby dismissal of rules

[handwritten note, bottom:] → Necissity conpells a prince to act unvirtuosly

not be good. But since men are a wicked lot and will not keep their promises to you, you likewise need not keep yours to them. A prince never lacks legitimate reasons to colour over his failure to keep his word.* Of this, one could cite an endless number of modern examples to show how many pacts and how many promises have been made null and void because of the faithlessness of princes; and he who has known best how to use the ways of the fox has come out best. But it is necessary to know how to colour over this nature effectively, and to be a great pretender and dissembler. Men are so simple-minded and so controlled by their immediate needs that he who deceives will always find someone who will let himself be deceived.

I do not wish to remain silent about one of these recent examples. Alexander VI never did anything else, nor thought about anything else, than to deceive men, and he always found someone to whom he could do this. There never has been a man who asserted anything with more effectiveness, nor whose affirmations rested upon greater oaths, who observed them less. Nevertheless, his deceptions always succeeded to his heart's desire, since he knew this aspect of the world very well.

Therefore, it is not necessary for a prince to possess all of the above-mentioned qualities, but it is very necessary for him to appear to possess them. Furthermore, I shall dare to assert this: that having them and always observing them is harmful, but appearing to observe them is useful: for instance, to appear merciful, faithful, humane, trustworthy, religious, and to be so; but with his mind disposed in such a way that, should it become necessary not to be so, he will be able and know how to change to the opposite. One must understand this: a prince, and especially a new prince, cannot observe all those things for which men are considered good, because in order to maintain the state he must often act against his faith, against charity, against humanity, and against religion. And so it is necessary that he should have a mind ready to turn itself according to the way the winds of Fortune and the changing circumstances command him. And, as I said above, he should not depart from the good if it is possible to do so, but he should know how to enter into evil when forced by necessity.

Therefore, a prince must be very careful never to let anything
fall from his lips that is not imbued with the five qualities mentioned above; to those seeing and hearing him, he should appear
to be all mercy, all faithfulness, all integrity, all humanity, and all
religion. And there is nothing more necessary than to seem to
possess this last quality. Men in general judge more by their eyes
than their hands: everyone can see, but few can feel. Everyone
sees what you seem to be, few touch upon what you are, and those
few do not dare to contradict the opinion of the many who have
the majesty of the state to defend them. In the actions of all men,
and especially of princes, where there is no tribunal to which to
appeal, one must consider the final result.* Therefore, let a prince
conquer and maintain the state, and his methods will always be
judged honourable and praised by all. For ordinary people are
always taken in by appearances and by the outcome of an event.
And in the world there are only ordinary people; and the few have
no place, while the many have a spot on which to lean. A certain
prince of the present times, whom it is best not to name,*
preaches nothing but peace and faith, and to both one and the
other he is extremely hostile. If he had observed both peace and
faith, he would have had either his reputation or his state taken
away from him many times over.

XIX
Of avoiding being despised and hated
[*De contemptu et odio fugiendo*]

BUT since I have spoken about the most important of the qualities
mentioned above, I should like to discuss the others briefly under
this general rule: that the prince, as was noted above, should
concentrate upon avoiding those things that make him hated and
contemptible. When he has avoided this, he will have carried out
his duties, and none of his other infamous deeds will cause him
any danger at all. As I have said, what makes him hated above all
else is being rapacious and a usurper of the property and the

women of his subjects. He must refrain from this. In most cases, so long as you do not deprive them of either their honour or their property, most men live content, and you only have to contend with the ambition of the few, who can be restrained without difficulty and by many means. What makes him despised is being considered changeable, frivolous, effeminate, cowardly, and irresolute. From these qualities, a prince must guard himself as if from a reef, and he must strive to make everyone recognize in his actions greatness, spirit, dignity, and strength. Concerning the private affairs of his subjects, he must insist that his decisions be irrevocable. And he should maintain this reputation in such a way that no man can imagine he is able to deceive or trick him.

That prince who creates such an opinion of himself has a great reputation; and it is difficult to conspire against a man with such a reputation and difficult to attack him, provided that he is understood to be of great ability and revered by his subjects. For a prince should have two fears: one internal, concerning his subjects; the other external, concerning foreign powers. From the latter, he can defend himself by his effective arms and his effective allies, and he will always have effective allies if he has effective arms. Internal affairs will always be stable when external affairs are stable, provided that they are not already disturbed by a conspiracy. And even if external conditions change, if he is properly organized and lives as I have said, and does not lose control of himself, he will always be able to withstand every attack, just as I said that Nabis the Spartan did.

But concerning his subjects, when external affairs do not change, he has to fear that they may be plotting in secret. The prince will protect himself against this danger by avoiding being either hated or despised and by keeping the people satisfied with him. It is essential to do this, as was discussed at length earlier. One of the most powerful remedies a prince has against conspiracies is not to be hated by the people, for whoever plans a conspiracy always believes that he will satisfy the people by killing the prince. But when he thinks he might injure them, he cannot summon the courage to undertake such a deed, for the problems on the part of the conspirators are countless. Experience demonstrates that there have been many conspiracies, but that few had a good end.* Anyone who conspires cannot act alone, nor can he find companions except from amongst those whom he believes to be discontented. As soon as you have revealed your intention to one malcontent, you give him the means to make himself content, since he can have everything he desires by revealing the plot. This is so much the case that, seeing a sure gain on the one hand, and one that is doubtful and full of danger on the other, if he is to remain loyal to you he must either be a rare kind of friend or a wholly obstinate enemy of the prince. Reducing the matter to a few brief words, let me say that on the part of the conspirator there is nothing but fear, apprehension, and the terrifying thought of punishment. But on the part of the prince there is the majesty of the principality, the laws, and the defences of friends and the state to protect him. And so, with the good will of the people added to all these things, it is impossible for anyone to be so rash as to plan a conspiracy, for where a conspirator usually has to be afraid before he executes his evil deed, in this case, having the people as an enemy, he must be afraid even afterwards, when the excess has occurred, nor can he hope to find any refuge because of this.

One could cite countless examples on this subject, but I shall be satisfied with only the one that occurred during the time of our fathers. The Canneschi family who conspired against him murdered Messer Annibale Bentivoglio, Prince of Bologna and grandfather of the present Messer Annibale. He left behind no heir except Messer Giovanni, then only in swaddling clothes. As soon as this murder occurred, the people rose up and killed all the Canneschi. This happened because of the good will that the house of the Bentivoglio enjoyed in those days. This good will was so great that, with Annibale dead and no one of that family left in the city who could rule Bologna, having heard that in Florence there was one of the Bentivoglio bloodline who was believed until that time to be the son of a blacksmith, the Bolognese people went to Florence to find him,* and they gave him the control of the city. He ruled it until Messer Giovanni came of age to rule.

I conclude, therefore, that a prince should not be too concerned about conspiracies when the people are well disposed toward him, but that when they are hostile and regard him with hatred, he must fear everything and everyone. Well-organized states and wise princes have taken great care not to drive the nobles to desperation and to satisfy the people and keep them contented, for this is one of the most important matters that concerns a prince.

Among the kingdoms that are well organized and well governed in our times is that of France. In it one finds countless good institutions upon which the liberty and the security of the king depend. Of these, the foremost is the parliament and its authority. For he who organized that kingdom—recognizing the ambition of the nobles and their insolence, and being aware of the necessity of keeping a bit in their mouths to hold them back, on the one hand; while on the other, knowing the hatred of the people for the nobles, based upon fear, and wanting to reassure them—did not wish this to be the particular concern of the king. In order to relieve himself of the blame he might incur from the nobles if he supported the common people, and from the common people if he supported the nobles, he therefore established a third judicial body that might restrain the nobles and favour the lower classes without burdening the king. There could be no better or more prudent an institution than this, nor could there be a better explanation for the security of the king and the kingdom. From this one can extract another notable observation: princes must delegate distasteful tasks to others, while pleasant ones they should keep for themselves. Again, I conclude that a prince must respect the nobles but not make himself hated by the people.

Perhaps it may seem to many who have studied the lives and deaths of some Roman emperors* that they provide examples contrary to this opinion of mine. For we discover that some of them always lived nobly and demonstrated great strength of character, yet nevertheless lost their empire or were killed by their own soldiers who plotted against them. Wishing, therefore, to reply to these objections, I shall discuss the characteristics of several emperors, showing the reasons for their downfall, which are not different from those that I myself have already presented. And in part I shall offer for consideration those things that are worthy of note for anyone who reads the history of those times. I shall let it suffice to choose all those emperors who succeeded to the throne from Marcus the philosopher to Maximinus: these were Marcus, his son Commodus, Pertinax, Julian, Severus, Antoninus Caracalla his son, Macrinus, Heliogabalus, Alexander, and Maximinus. It is first to be noted that, while in other principalities one has only to contend with the ambition of the nobles and the insolence of the people, the Roman emperors had a third problem: they had to endure the cruelty and avarice of the soldiers. This created such difficulties that it was the cause of the downfall of many of them, since it was difficult to satisfy both the soldiers and the people. The people loved peace and quiet and, because of this, they were pleased by decent princes, while the soldiers loved a prince with military spirit who was cruel, arrogant, and rapacious. They wanted him to exercise such qualities on the people, so that they might double their salary and give vent to their avarice and cruelty. These things always brought about the downfall of those emperors who, by nature or experience, did not have so great a reputation that they could keep both the people and the soldiers in check. Most of them, especially those who came to the principality as new men, when they recognized the difficulty resulting from the two opposing humours, turned to appeasing the soldiers, caring little about injuring the people. Such a course of action was necessary, and since princes cannot avoid being hated by somebody, they must first seek not to be hated by the largest group. When they cannot do this, they must try with every effort to avoid the hatred of the most powerful group. And so those emperors who had need of extraordinary support because of their newness in power allied themselves with the soldiers rather than the people. Nevertheless, whether this proved to their advantage or not depended on whether the prince knew how to maintain his reputation with the soldiers.

For the reasons discussed above, it came about that, of Marcus, Pertinax, and Alexander—who all lived decent lives, were lovers of justice, enemies of cruelty, humane, and kindly—all except

Marcus came to a bad end. Marcus alone lived and died with the greatest honour, for he succeeded to the empire by right of birth, and he did not have to recognize any obligation for it either to the soldiers or the people. Then, being endowed with many virtues that made him venerable, while he was alive he always held both the one order and the other within their limits, and he was never either hated or despised. But Pertinax was made emperor against the will of the soldiers, who, accustomed to living licentiously under Commodus, could not tolerate the honest way of life to which Pertinax wished to return them. Therefore, having made himself hated, and since to this hatred was added contempt for his old age, Pertinax came to ruin at the very outset of his rule. Here, one must note that hatred is acquired just as much through good actions as by sorry ones. And so, as I said above, if a prince wishes to maintain the state, he is often obliged not to be good, because whenever that group you believe you need to support you is corrupted—whether it be the people, the soldiers, or the nobles—it is to your advantage to follow their inclinations in order to satisfy them, and then good deeds are your enemy.

But let us come to Alexander. He was of such goodness that among the other laudable deeds attributed to him is this: in the fourteen years he ruled the empire, he never put anyone to death without a trial. Nevertheless, since he was considered effeminate and a man who let himself be controlled by his mother, he was despised, and as a result the army plotted against him and murdered him.

Considering now, in contrast, the characteristics of Commodus, Severus, Antoninus Caracalla, and Maximinus, you will find them extremely cruel and extremely rapacious. In order to satisfy their soldiers, they did not hesitate to inflict all kinds of injuries upon the people. All except Severus came to a sorry end. For in Severus there was so much virtue that, keeping the soldiers as his allies even though the people were oppressed by him, he was always able to rule happily, since those abilities of his made him so admired in the eyes of both the soldiers and the people that the former were awestruck and stupefied and the latter were respectful and satisfied. And since the actions of this man were grand and noteworthy for a new prince, I should like to demonstrate briefly how well he knew how to play the role of the lion and the fox, whose natures, as I say above, a prince must imitate.

As soon as Severus learned of the indecisiveness of the emperor Julian, he convinced the army of which he was in command in Slavonia that it would be a good idea to march to Rome to avenge the death of Pertinax, who had been murdered by the Praetorian Guards. Under this pretext,* without showing his aspiration for imperial power, he moved his army to Rome, and was in Italy before his departure was known. When he arrived in Rome the Senate elected him emperor out of fear, and put Julian to death. After this beginning, there remained two problems for Severus if he wanted to make himself master of the entire state. The first was in Asia, where Pescennius Niger, commander of the Asian armies, had himself proclaimed emperor. The other was in the West, where Albinus was, who also aspired to imperial power. And since Severus judged it dangerous to reveal himself as an enemy to both of them, he decided to attack Pescennius Niger and to trick Albinus. To the latter he wrote that, having been elected emperor by the Senate, he wanted to share that honour with him, and he sent him the title of Caesar and, by decree of the Senate, made him his coequal. These things were accepted by Albinus as the truth. But after Severus had conquered and executed Pescennius Niger and had pacified affairs in the East, upon returning to Rome he complained to the Senate that Albinus, ungrateful for the benefits received from him, had treacherously sought to kill him, and for this he was obliged to go and punish his ingratitude. Then he went to find him in France, and took both his state and his life. Anyone, therefore, who examines in detail the actions of this man, will find him both a very ferocious lion and a very shrewd fox. He will see him feared and respected by everyone, and not hated by his armies. And one should not be amazed that he, a new man, was able to hold on to such imperial power, because his outstanding reputation always defended him from the hatred that the people might have felt for him on account of his plundering.

But his son Antoninus was also a man who had excellent

qualities that made him greatly admired in the view of the people and pleasing to the soldiers, for he was a military man, well able to bear up under any kind of hardship, a despiser of all delicate foods and every other kind of soft living, and this made him loved by the armies. Nevertheless, his ferocity and cruelty were so great and so unheard of—since, after countless individual killings, he had put to death a large part of the populace of Rome and all that of Alexandria*—that he became intensely hated all over the world. He also began to be feared even by those he kept around him, so that a centurion murdered him in the midst of his army. From this, it is to be noted that such deaths as these, that result from the deliberation of a man of obstinate spirit, are unavoidable for princes, since anyone who does not fear death can injure them. But the prince must not be too afraid of such men, for they are extremely rare. He must only guard against inflicting serious injury on anyone who serves him and anyone he has near him in the service of his principality, as Antoninus had done. Antoninus had shamefully put to death that centurion's brother, and he threatened the man every day, yet he kept him as a bodyguard. This was a rash decision and, as it happened, one that brought about his downfall.

But let us come to Commodus, who held imperial power with great ease, having inherited it by birth, being the son of Marcus. It would have been enough for him to follow in the footsteps of his father, and he would have satisfied the soldiers and the people. But having a cruel and bestial spirit, in order to practise his greed upon the people, he turned to pleasing the armies and to making them undisciplined. On the other hand, by not maintaining his dignity, frequently descending into the arenas to fight with the gladiators and doing other degrading things unworthy of the imperial majesty, he became contemptible in the sight of the soldiers. Being hated on the one hand and despised on the other, he was plotted against and murdered.

The qualities of Maximinus remain to be described. He was a very warlike man. Because the armies were angered by Alexander's softness, which I discussed above, after Alexander's death they elected him to imperial power. He did not retain it very long, for two things made him hated and contemptible. The first was very base birth, having once herded sheep in Thrace. This fact was well known everywhere and caused him to lose considerable dignity in everyone's eyes. The second was that at the beginning of his reign he deferred going to Rome to take possession of the imperial throne, and he had established the reputation of being very cruel, having committed many cruel deeds through his prefects in Rome and in all other parts of the empire. As a result, the entire world was moved by disgust at the baseness of his blood and by the hatred caused by fear of his cruelty. First Africa rebelled, then the Senate with the entire populace of Rome, and finally all of Italy conspired against him. To this was added even his own army, for while besieging Aquileia and finding the capture difficult, disgusted by his cruelty and fearing him less, seeing that Maximinus had many enemies, the soldiers murdered him.

I do not wish to discuss Heliogabalus or Macrinus or Julian, who were immediately wiped out since they were universally contemptible. But I shall come to the conclusion of this discourse. Let me say that the princes of our times, in their governance, suffer less from this problem of satisfying their soldiers by extraordinary means. Although they have to consider them to some extent, yet they resolve the question quickly, for none of these princes has standing armies that have evolved along with the government and the administration of their territory, as did the armies of the Roman Empire. And therefore, if it was then necessary to satisfy the soldiers more than the people, that was because the soldiers could do more than the people. Now it is more necessary for all princes, except the Turk and the Sultan,* to satisfy the people more than the soldiers, since the people can do more than the soldiers. I make an exception of the Turk, for he always maintains near him twelve thousand infantrymen and fifteen thousand cavalrymen, upon whom depend the safety and the strength of his kingdom, and it is necessary that this ruler should maintain them as his allies, setting aside all other concerns. Likewise, as the kingdom of the Sultan lies entirely in the hands of the soldiers, it is fitting that he too should maintain them as his allies, without considering the people. And you must note that this state of the Sultan is unlike all the other principalities, since it is similar to the Christian pontificate, which cannot be called either a hereditary principality or a new principality. For it is not the sons of the old prince who are the heirs and then become its rulers, but rather the one who is elected to that rank by those who have the authority to do so. Because this institution is an ancient one, it cannot be called a new principality. In it are none of those difficulties that are encountered in new ones, for although the prince is new, the institutions of that state are old and are organized to receive him as if he were their hereditary ruler.

But let us return to our topic. Let me say that anyone who considers the discourse written above will see how either hatred or contempt has been the cause of the downfall of these previously mentioned emperors. He will also recognize how it comes to pass that, in each of these groups, one man had a happy ending and the others an unhappy one, although some acted in one way and others in a contrary manner. Since they were new princes, it was useless and damaging for Pertinax and Alexander to wish to imitate Marcus, who was installed in the principality by right of birth. Likewise, it was disastrous for Caracalla, Commodus, and Maximinus to imitate Severus, since they did not have enough virtue to follow in his footsteps. Therefore, a new prince in a new principality cannot imitate the deeds of Marcus, not yet does he need to follow those of Severus. Instead, he should take from Severus those qualities that are necessary to found his state, and from Marcus those that are suitable and glorious in order to conserve a state that is already established and stable.

[handwritten marginal note: Church as government again]

XX

Of whether fortresses and many things that princes employ every day are useful or harmful

[*An arces et multa alia, quae quotidie a principibus fiunt, utilia an inutilia sint*]

SOME princes have disarmed their subjects in order to hold the state securely. Others have kept their conquered lands divided. Some have encouraged hostilities against themselves. Others have turned to winning the support of those who were suspect at the beginning of their rule. Some have built fortresses; others have torn them down and destroyed them. And although one cannot render a precise judgement concerning these matters without knowing the particular details of those states where some similar decision had to be taken, nevertheless I shall speak in as broad a manner as the subject-matter will allow.

Now, there has never been a time when a new prince disarmed his subjects. On the contrary, when he has found them unarmed, he has always armed them, because when armed those arms become yours: those whom you suspect become loyal, and those who were loyal remain so, and they become your partisans rather than your subjects. Since all of your subjects cannot be armed, when those you arm receive benefits, you can deal more securely with the others. The difference in treatment toward themselves that they recognize makes them obligated to you. The others excuse you, judging it necessary that those who are in more danger and who hold more responsibility should have a greater reward. But when you disarm them you begin to offend them. You show that you distrust them, either for cowardice or for lack of loyalty. And both of these opinions generate hatred against you. Since you cannot be unarmed, you will have to turn to mercenary soldiers, who have the characteristics explained above. And even if they were good, they could not be strong enough to defend you from powerful enemies and from disloyal subjects.

Therefore, as I have said, a new prince in a new principality has always instituted an army, and the history books are filled with such examples. But when a prince acquires a new state that is joined to his old one like an appendage,* then it is necessary to disarm that state, except for those who have been your partisans in its acquisition. And they as well, with time and the appropriate opportunity, must be rendered weak and effeminate, and things must be organized in such a way that the armed strength of your entire state will be concentrated in your own troops who live near you in your older state.

Our ancestors and those who were considered wise used to say that it was necessary to hold Pistoia by factions and Pisa by fortresses. Because of this, they would encourage factional strife in some of their subject towns in order to control them more easily. During those times when Italy enjoyed a balance of power* to a certain extent, this advice may have been a good policy. But I do not believe that it can be given as a rule today, since I do not think that factions ever did any good. On the contrary, when the enemy approaches, divided cities are always immediately lost. The weaker factions will always join the external forces, and the others will not be able to stand up to them. Moved by the reasons stated above, I believe, the Venetians encouraged the Guelf and Ghibelline sects* in their subject cities. Although they never permitted matters to come to bloodshed, they still fostered these quarrels between them so that those citizens would not unite against them, being busy with their own disputes. As we have seen, this policy did not turn out as they had planned. For after their defeat at Vailà,* one faction of these cities was immediately emboldened and seized the entire territory* from them. Methods such as these, moreover, are signs of weakness in a prince. In a strong principality such factions will never be allowed, since they are profitable only in peacetime, allowing the subjects to be more easily manipulated by such means; but when war comes, such arrangements reveal their fallacious nature.

Without a doubt, princes become great when they overcome difficulties and obstacles imposed upon them. And therefore, Fortune—especially when she wishes to increase the reputation

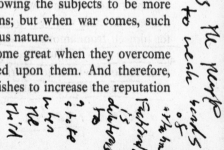

of a new prince, who has a greater need to acquire reputation than a hereditary prince does—creates enemies for him, and has them undertake enterprises against him so that he will have the chance to overcome them and to climb higher up the ladder his enemies have brought him. Thus, many people judge that a wise prince must cunningly foster some hostile action, whenever he has the opportunity, so that in repressing it his greatness will emerge all the more.

Princes, especially those that are new, have discovered more loyalty and more utility in those men who, at the beginning of their rule, were considered suspect than in those who were trusted at first. Pandolfo Petrucci, Prince of Siena, ruled his state more with the assistance of men who had been held in suspicion than by others. But on this issue one cannot speak in generalities, for the situation varies according to the case. I shall only say this: the prince will always easily win the support of those men who have been enemies at the beginning of the principality, the kind of men who must have support in order to maintain themselves. They are even more obliged to serve him loyally, inasmuch as they recognize the need to cancel the suspicious opinion the prince had of them through their deeds. And thus the prince will always derive more profit from them than from those who neglect his affairs and serve him with too much self-confidence.

Since the subject requires it, I do not wish to fail to remind princes who have recently conquered a state by means of assistance from its inhabitants to consider carefully what reason may have moved those who have supported them to support them. If it is not natural affection for him, but simply because they were unhappy with the preceding state, he will be able to keep them as his allies only with hard work and the greatest of difficulty, since it will be impossible for him to satisfy them. Carefully considering the reason for this, with examples drawn from ancient and modern times, it will be seen that he can more easily win friends for himself from amongst those men who were content with the preceding state, and who were therefore his enemies, rather than from those who became his friends and helped him to occupy the state because they were not satisfied with it.

More inertia

In order to hold their states more securely, princes have been accustomed to erect fortresses that may serve as the bridle and bit for those who might plot an attack against them, and to have a secure shelter from a sudden attack. I praise this method, because it has been employed since ancient times. Nevertheless, in our own times Messer Niccolò Vitelli was seen to demolish two fortresses in Città del Castello in order to hold that state.* Guido Ubaldo, Duke of Urbino, completely razed to the foundations all the fortresses of that territory after returning to the rule from which Cesare Borgia had driven him, and he decided that without them it would be more difficult to recapture that state.* The Bentivoglio family took similar measures after returning to power in Bologna.* Fortresses, then, are either useful or not, depending upon the times: if they benefit you in one way, they injure you in another. This argument may be dealt with as follows: the prince who is more afraid of his people than of foreigners should build fortresses, but one who is more afraid of foreigners than of his people should do without them. The castle of Milan that Francesco Sforza built there* has caused and will cause more wars against the Sforza family than any other disorder in that state. However, the best fortress that exists is not to be hated by the people. Although you may have fortresses, they will not save you if the people hate you, for once the people have taken up arms, they never lack for foreigners who will assist them. In our times, we have not seen that they have benefited any prince except the Countess of Forlì, after her consort, Count Girolamo, was killed. Because of her castle, she was able to escape the popular uprising and to wait until help arrived from Milan in order to regain her state.* The times were such at that moment that no foreigner could give assistance to her people. But later on, fortresses were of little value to her when Cesare Borgia attacked her and when her hostile populace joined with the foreigner. Then and earlier, therefore, it would have been safer for her not to be hated by her people than to have had the fortresses. Considering all these matters, then, I shall praise both those princes who construct fortresses and those who do not. And I shall reproach any prince who, trusting in fortresses, considers the hatred of the people to be of little importance.

XXI

How a prince should act to acquire esteem
[*Quod principem deceat ut egregious habeatur*]

NOTHING makes a prince more esteemed than great undertakings and showing himself to be extraordinary. In our own
times we have Ferdinand of Aragon, the present King of Spain.
This man can be called almost a new prince, since from being a
weak ruler, through fame and glory he became the first king of
Christendom. If you consider his deeds you will find them all
very grand, and some even extraordinary. In the beginning of his
reign he attacked Granada,* and that enterprise was the basis of
his state. First, he acted while things were peaceful and when he
had no fear of opposition. He kept the minds of the barons of
Castile occupied with this, so that, concentrating on that war,
they did not consider rebellion. In this way he acquired reputation and dominion over them without their noticing it. He was
able to maintain armies with money from the Church and the
people, and through that long war he laid a basis for his own
army, which has since brought him honour.* Besides this, in
order to be able to undertake great enterprises, he had recourse to
a pious cruelty, always employing religion for his own purposes,*
chasing the Marranos out of his kingdom and seizing their property.* No example of his actions could be more pathetic or more
extraordinary than this. He attacked Africa* under the same cloak
of religion. He undertook the invasion of Italy.* Lately, he
attacked France.* And thus he has always accomplished and
organized great deeds, that have always kept the minds of his
subjects surprised, amazed, and occupied with their outcome.
One action of his would spring from another in such a way that,
between one and the other, he would never give men enough time
to be able to work calmly against him.

It also helps a prince a great deal to show himself to be extraordinary in dealing with internal affairs, as in the reports about

Messer Bernabò Visconti of Milan.* When the occasion arises that a person in public life performs some extraordinary act, be it good or evil, the prince should find a way of rewarding or punishing him that will provoke a great deal of discussion. And above all, a prince should strive in all of his actions to achieve the reputation of a great man of outstanding intelligence.

A prince is also respected when he is a true friend and a true enemy: that is, when he declares himself to be on the side of one prince against another, without reserve. Such a policy will always be more useful than remaining neutral, for if two powerful neighbours of yours come to blows, they will be of the kind that, when one has emerged victorious, you will either have cause to fear the victor or you will not. In either of these two cases, it will always be more useful for you to declare yourself and to wage open warfare. In the first case, if you do not disclose your intentions you will always be the prey of whoever wins, to the delight and satisfaction of whoever loses, and you will have no reason at all why anyone should come to your assistance or take you in. Because whoever wins does not want reluctant allies who would not assist him in times of adversity; whoever loses will not give you refuge, since you were unwilling to run the risk of sharing his fortune.

Antiochus came into Greece, sent there by the Aetolians to drive out the Romans. Antiochus sent ambassadors to the Achaeans, who were allies of the Romans, to encourage them to remain neutral. On the other hand, the Romans urged them to take up arms with them. This matter came up for debate in the council of the Achaeans, where the legate of Antiochus persuaded them to remain neutral. To this the Roman legate replied: 'Quod autem isti dicunt, non interponendi vos bello, nihil magis alienum rebus vestries est: sine gratia, sine dignitate premium vitoris eritis'* ['The counsel these men give you about not entering the war is indeed contrary to your interests: without respect and dignity, you will be the prey of the victors']. It will always happen that he who is not your friend will request your neutrality, and he who is your friend will ask you to disclose your intentions by taking up arms. In order to avoid present dangers, irresolute princes follow the neutral path most of the time, and most of the time they come to ruin. But when the prince declares himself energetically in favour of one side, if the one with whom you have joined wins, he has an obligation towards you and there exists a bond of affection between you, although he may be powerful and you may be left in his power. Men are never so dishonest that they will repress an ally with such a flagrant display of ingratitude. Nor are victories ever so clear-cut that the victor can be completely free of concern, especially for justice. But if the one with whom you join loses, you can be given refuge by him, and while he is able to do so, he can help you, and you will become the comrade of a fortune that may flourish again.

In the second case, when those who fight together are such that you need not fear the one who wins, it is even more prudent to take sides; since you achieve the downfall of one prince with the aid of another, who should have saved him if he had been wise; and who, once he has won, remains at your discretion—and it is impossible for him not to win, with your help. Here it is to be noted that a prince must avoid ever joining forces with one more powerful than himself to injure others, unless necessity compels you, as was mentioned above. For if you win you remain his prisoner, and princes should avoid being left at the discretion of others as much as possible. The Venetians allied themselves with France against the Duke of Milan,* and they could have avoided that alliance: it resulted in their downfall.* But when such an alliance cannot be avoided, as happened to the Florentines when the Pope and Spain went with their armies to attack Lombardy,* then a prince should join for the reasons given above. Nor should any state ever believe that it can always choose safe courses of action. On the contrary, it should recognize that they will all be risky, for we find this to be in the order of things: that whenever we try to avoid one disadvantage, we run into another. Prudence consists in knowing how to recognize the nature of disadvantages, and how to choose the least sorry one as good.

A prince should also demonstrate that he is a lover of the virtues,* by giving hospitality to virtuous men and by honouring those who excel in a particular skill.* Furthermore, he should encourage his subjects to pursue their trades in tranquillity, whether in commerce, agriculture, or in any other human pursuit. No one should be afraid to increase his property for fear that it will be taken away from him, while no one should shrink from undertaking any business through fear of taxes. Instead, the prince must establish rewards for those who wish to do these things, and for anyone who seeks in any way to enrich his city or state.* Besides this, at the appropriate times of the year he should keep the populace occupied with festivals and spectacles. And because each city is divided into guilds* or neighbourhoods,* he should take account of these groups, meet with them on occasion, and offer himself as an example of humanity and munificence while always, nevertheless, firmly maintaining the majesty of his dignity.

XXII

Of the prince's private secretaries*

[*De his quos a secretis principes habent*]

THE selection of ministers is of no little importance to a prince; and they are good or not, according to the prince's prudence. The first thing one does to evaluate a ruler's prudence is to look at the men he has around him. When they are capable and loyal, one can always consider him wise, for he has known how to recognize their capacities and to keep them loyal; but when they are otherwise, one can always form a negative judgement of him, for the first error he makes is made in this selection.

There was no one who knew Messer Antonio da Venafro, minister to Pandolfo Petrucci, Prince of Siena, who did not judge Pandolfo to be a very worthy man for having him as his minister. There are three kinds of intelligence:* one understands on its own; the second discerns what others understand; and the third neither understands by itself nor through others. The first kind is most excellent, the second is excellent, and the third is useless. Therefore, it must have been the case that if Pandolfo's intelligence was not of the first rank, it had to be of the second; for whenever a man has the intelligence to recognize the good or evil that another man does and says, although he may not have such capacities himself, he recognizes the good and the sorry deeds of his minister, and praises the former and corrects the others; and the minister cannot hope to trick him, and so continues to act well.

But as to how a prince may recognize such a minister, there is this method that never fails. When you see that the minister thinks more about himself than about you, and that in all his deeds he seeks out his own interests, such a man as this will never be a good minister, and you will never be able to trust him. For a man who holds the state of another in his hands must never think about himself, but always about his prince, and he must never be concerned about anything that does not concern his prince. On the other hand, the prince should be mindful of the minister so as to keep him acting well, honouring him, making him rich, putting him in his debt, giving him a share of the honours and responsibilities; so that the minister recognizes that he cannot exist without the prince, so that the many honours he has prevent him desiring more, so that the abundance of his wealth will stop him desiring more riches, and so that his many offices will make him fearful of changes. Therefore, when ministers and princes are related in this way, they can trust each other. When they are otherwise, the outcome will always be harmful either for one or the other.

XXIII

Of how to avoid flatterers
[*Quomodo adulators sint fugiendi*]

I DO not wish to omit an important issue, and an error from which princes protect themselves with difficulty if they are not extremely prudent, or if they do not make good choices. And these are the flatterers, of which the courts are full.* Because men delight so much in their own concerns, deceiving themselves in this way, that they find it difficult to protect themselves from this pestilence; while wishing to defend oneself from it brings the danger of becoming despised. For there is no other way to guard yourself against flattery than by making men understand that by telling you the truth they will not injure you. But when anyone can tell you the truth, you lose respect. Therefore, a prudent prince should follow a third course, electing wise men for his state and giving only them permission to speak truthfully to him, and only on such matters as he asks them about and not on other subjects. But he should ask them about everything and should listen to their opinions, and afterwards he should deliberate by himself in his own way. And in such councils, and with each of his ministers, he should conduct himself in such a way that all will realize that the more freely they speak, the more they will please him. Apart from these, he should refuse to listen to anyone else, pursue his goals directly, and be obstinate in the decisions he has taken. Anyone who does otherwise either comes to ruin because of the flatterer, or keeps changing his mind in the face of different opinions; resulting in a low estimation of his worth.

In this regard, I wish to cite a modern example. In speaking about His Majesty, Father Luca, the present Emperor Maximilian's man, declared that the Emperor never sought advice from anyone, nor did he ever do anything in his own way. And this arose from his following a manner of thinking contrary to the one discussed above. Because the Emperor is a secretive man, he communicates his plans to no one, nor does he take their advice. However, when he is carrying out his plans and they begin to be recognized and uncovered, they begin to be criticized by those around him; and he, just as if it were a simple matter, lets himself be diverted. From this results the fact that those things he does one day, he undoes the next; and that no one ever understands what he wants or what plans he is making, and that no one can rely on his decisions.

Therefore, a prince should always seek advice, but when he wants to, and not when others wish it. On the contrary, he should discourage anyone from giving him advice unless he asks for it. But he should be a very frequent questioner, and then, concerning the matters inquired about, a patient listener to the truth. Indeed, if he learns that anyone, for any reason, is reluctant to speak to him, this should worry him. Although many feel that any prince who is considered prudent is reputed to be so not because of his own nature but because of the good counsellors he has around him, without a doubt they are deceived. For this is a general rule that never fails: a prince who is not wise on his own cannot be well advised, unless by chance he has submitted himself to a single person who governs him in everything and who is a most prudent man. In this case he could be well advised, but this would not last long, because such a governor would very soon take the state away from him. But if he seeks advice from more than one counsellor, a prince who is not wise will never have consistent advice, nor will he know how to make it consistent by himself. Each of his advisers will think about his own interests; the prince will not know either how to correct them or recognize them. One cannot find advisers who are any different, for men always turn out bad for you, unless some necessity makes them act well. Therefore, it is to be concluded that good advice, from whomever it may come, must arise from the prudence of the prince, and not the prudence of the prince from good advice.

XXIV

Why Italian princes have lost their states

[*Cur Italiae principes regnum amiserunt*]

IF followed prudently, the things written above make a new prince seem like a long-established one, and render him immediately more secure and settled in his state than if he had possessed it for a long time. For a new prince is far more closely observed in his actions than is a hereditary prince. When his actions are recognized as skilful, they strike men much more and bind them to him more strongly than does antiquity of bloodline. For men are much more taken by present concerns than by those of the past, and when they discover benefit in present things, they enjoy it and seek no more. In fact, they will seize every measure to defend the new prince so long as he is not neglectful of his duties. Thus, he will have the double glory of having founded a new principality, and of having adorned and furnished it with good laws, good armies, and good actions; just as he is doubly shameful who, being born a prince, loses his principality because of his lack of prudence.

If one considers those Italian lords who have lost their states in our times, such as the King of Naples, the Duke of Milan,* and others, one first discovers in them a common defect insofar as armies are concerned, for the reasons that were discussed at length above. Then one sees some of them who either had the people against them, or if the people were friendly towards them, they did not know how to protect themselves from the nobles. Without these defects, states that have enough strength* to take an army into the field are not lost. Philip of Macedon—not the father of Alexander, but the man defeated by Titus Quinctius*—did not have much of a state compared to the great power of the Romans and Greeks who attacked him. Nonetheless, because he was a military man and knew how to win the people over and to secure himself against the nobility, he succeeded in waging war against them for many years. And if finally he lost dominion over a few cities, his kingdom nevertheless remained.*

Therefore, these princes of ours who have ruled their principalities for many years and who have subsequently lost them should not blame Fortune, but rather their own indolence. Since in peaceful times they never imagined that things might change—not to consider the possibility of a storm in good weather is a common defect among men—when adverse times finally arrived, they thought about running away and not about defending themselves. They hoped that, angered by the insolence of the victors, the people would call them back. When no other plans exist, this is a good one; but it is very bad to have disregarded all other remedies for this one. You should never wish to fall down, in the belief that you will find someone to pick you up. This may not happen, but even if it does it will not increase your security, since it is a vile kind of defence, and is not under your control.

Only those defences that depend on you yourself and on your own virtue are good, certain, and lasting.

[handwritten: Self-sufficiency is the only certainty]

XXV

Of Fortune's power in human affairs and how she can be resisted

*[Quantum Fortuna in rebus humanis posit et quomodo
illi sit occurrendum]*

I AM not unaware that many have held, and do still hold, the opinion that the affairs of this world are controlled by Fortune and by God, that men cannot control them with their prudence, and that, on the contrary, men can have no remedy whatsoever for them. For this reason, they might judge that it is useless to lose much sweat over such matters, and let them be controlled by fate. This opinion has been held all the more in our own times because of the enormous upheavals that have been observed and are being observed every day—events beyond human conjecture. When I have thought about it, sometimes I am inclined to a certain degree towards their opinion. Nevertheless, in order not to wipe out our free will, I consider it to be true that Fortune is the arbiter of one half of our actions, but that she still leaves the control of the other half, or almost that, to us.* I compare her to one of those destructive rivers that, when they become enraged, flood the plains, ruin the trees and buildings, raising the earth from one spot and dropping it onto another. Everyone flees before it; everyone yields to its impetus, unable to oppose it in any way. But although rivers are like this, it does not mean that we cannot take precautions with dikes and dams when the weather is calm, so that when they rise up again either the waters will be channelled off or their force will be neither so damaging nor so out of control. The same things occur where Fortune is concerned. She shows her power where there is no well-ordered virtue* to resist her, and therefore turns her impetus towards where she knows no

[handwritten margin note: More of a share than Alberti gives]

dikes and dams have been constructed to hold her in. If you consider Italy, the seat of these upheavals and the area which has set them in motion, you will see a countryside without dikes and without a single dam: if Italy had been protected with proper virtue, as is the case in Germany, Spain, and France, either this flood would not have produced the enormous upheavals that it has, or it would not have struck here at all. And with this I consider I have said enough about resisting Fortune in general.

Restricting myself more to particulars, let me say that one sees a prince prospering today and coming to ruin tomorrow without having seen him change his nature or his qualities. I believe this happens first because of the causes that have been discussed at length earlier. That is, that the prince who relies completely upon Fortune will come to ruin as soon as she changes. I also believe that the man who adapts his method of procedure to the nature of the times will prosper, and likewise, that the man who establishes his procedures out of tune with the times will come to grief. We can observe in the affairs that lead them to the end they seek— that is, towards glory and wealth—that men proceed in different ways: one man with caution, another with impetuousness; one with violence, another with astuteness; one with patience, another with its opposite. Each may achieve his goals with these different means. In the case of two cautious men, we also see that one reaches his goal while the other does not. And likewise, two men prosper equally employing two different means, one being cautious and the other impetuous. This occurs from nothing other than from the quality of the times, that either match or do not match their procedures. This follows from what I said: two men acting differently can reach the same result; and of two men acting identically, one reaches his goal and the other does not. On this also depends the variation of the good,* for if a man governs himself with caution and patience, while the times and circumstances are turning in such a way that his conduct is appropriate, he will prosper. But if the times and circumstances change he will be ruined, because he does not change his method of procedure. No man is so prudent that he knows how to adapt himself to this fact, both because he cannot deviate from that to which he is by nature inclined, and also because he cannot be persuaded to depart from a path after having always prospered by following it. And therefore, when it is time to act impetuously the cautious man does not know how to do so, and is ruined as a result; for if he had changed his conduct with the times, Fortune would not have changed.

Pope Julius II acted impetuously in all his affairs, and he found the times and circumstances so suitable to this method of procedure that he always achieved felicitous results. Consider the first campaign he waged against Bologna while Messer Giovanni Bentivoglio was still alive.* The Venetians were unhappy about it and so was the King of Spain. Julius still had negotiations going on about it with France. Nevertheless, he started personally on this expedition with his usual ferocity and impetuosity. Such a move astonished Spain and the Venetians and stopped them in their tracks, the latter out of fear and the former out of a desire to recover the entire Kingdom of Naples. On the other hand, Julius involved the King of France, for when the King saw him move, and wishing to make him his ally in order to defeat the Venetians, the King decided that he could not deny the Pope the use of his troops without openly injuring him. Therefore, with his impetuous move, Julius accomplished what no other pontiff would ever have achieved with the greatest of human prudence. For if he had waited until he could leave Rome with agreements settled and everything in order, as any other pontiff would have done, he would never have succeeded, because the King of France would have found a thousand excuses and the others would have aroused in him a thousand fears. I wish to leave unmentioned the other deeds of his, since all were similar and all succeeded well. The brevity of his life* did not allow him to experience the contrary; since if times that required proceeding with caution had arrived, his ruin would have followed, for he would never have deviated from those methods to which his nature inclined him.

I therefore conclude that, since Fortune varies and men remain obstinate in their ways, men prosper when the two are in harmony* and fail to prosper when they are not in accord. I certainly believe this: that it is better to be impetuous than cautious, because Fortune is a woman, and if you want to keep her under it is necessary to beat her and force her down. It is clear that she more often allows herself to be won over by impetuous men than by those who proceed coldly. And so, like a woman, Fortune is always the friend of young men, for they are less cautious, more ferocious, and command her with more audacity.

XXVI

An exhortation to seize Italy and to free her from the barbarians

[Exortatio ad capessendam Italiam in libertatemque a barbaris vindicandam]

THEREFORE, considering all of the matters discussed above, and wondering to myself whether at present in Italy the times are suitable to honour a new prince, and if there is the material that might give a prudent and virtuous prince the opportunity to introduce a form that would do him honour and bring benefit to the people of Italy, it seems to me that so many circumstances are favourable to such a new prince that I know of no other time more appropriate to this. And if, as I said, it was necessary for the people of Israel to be enslaved in Egypt to make known the virtue of Moses, and it was necessary for the Persians to be oppressed by the Medes to make known the greatness of spirit in Cyrus, and it was necessary for the Athenians to be scattered to make known the excellence of Theseus, then at present, to make known the virtue of an Italian spirit, it was necessary for Italy to be reduced to her present conditions, and that she be more enslaved than the Hebrews, more servile than the Persians, and more scattered than the Athenians: without a leader, without order, beaten, despoiled, ripped apart, overrun, and having suffered every sort of ruin.

And even though, before now, some glimmer of light may have shown itself in a single individual,* so that it was possible to believe that God had ordained him for Italy's redemption, yet afterwards it was seen how, at the height of his deeds, he was rejected by Fortune. Now Italy, left as if lifeless, awaits the man who may heal her wounds and put an end to the plundering of Lombardy,* the extortions* in the Kingdom of Naples and in Tuscany, and who can cure her of those sores that have been festering for so long. Look how she now prays to God to send someone to redeem her from these barbaric cruelties and insults. See how ready and willing she is to follow a banner, provided that someone picks it up. Nor is there anyone in sight, at present, in whom she can have more hope than in Your Illustrious House, which, with its fortune and virtue, favoured by God and by the Church, of which it is now prince,* could place itself at the head of this redemption. This will not be very difficult if you keep before your eyes the deeds and the lives of those named above. Although those men were rare and marvellous, they were nevertheless men, and each of them had poorer opportunities than are offered now: for their undertakings were no more just, nor easier than this one, nor was God more a friend to them than to you. This is a righteous cause: 'iustum enim est bellum quibus necessarium et pia arma ubi nulla nisi in armis spes est'* ['Only those wars that are necessary are just, and arms are sacred when there is no hope except through arms']. Here circumstances are very favourable, and where circumstances are favourable there cannot be great difficulty, provided that you imitate the institutions of those men I have proposed as your target. Besides this, we now see here extraordinary, unprecedented signs brought about by God: the sea has opened up; a cloud has shown you the path; the rock has poured water forth; here manna has rained; everything has converged for your greatness.* The rest you must do yourself. God does not wish to do everything, in order not to take from us our free will and part of the glory that is ours.

It is not a marvel if some of the Italians mentioned previously were not capable of achieving what it is hoped Your Illustrious House may achieve, or that, during the many revolutions in Italy and the many wartime campaigns, it always seems that Italy's military skill has been wiped out. This arises from the fact that her ancient military practices were not good, and that there has existed nobody capable of inventing new ones. Nothing brings so much honour to a man newly risen up than the new laws and new institutions discovered by him. When these are well founded and have greatness in them, they make a man revered and admirable; and in Italy there is no lack of material for introducing every form there. Here there is great virtue in the limbs, were it not for the lack of it in the heads.* Observe how in duels and skirmishes Italians are superior in strength, dexterity, and resourcefulness. But when it comes to armies, they are not a match for others. All this comes from the weakness of her leaders, for those who know are not obeyed; and of each who thinks he knows, there has not been one up to the present day who has known how to set himself above the others, either because of virtue or fortune, so that others might yield to him. As a consequence, during so much time and so many wars waged during the past twenty years, whenever there has been an army made up completely of Italians it has always made a poor showing. As proof of this, there is Taro; then Alexandria, Capua, Genoa, Vailà, Bologna, and Mestre.*

Therefore, if Your Illustrious House desires to follow these excellent men who redeemed their countries, it is necessary before all else, and as a true basis for every enterprise, to provide yourself with your own soldiers, for one cannot have more loyal, or truer, or better soldiers. Although each one of them may be good individually, united together they will become even better, when they see themselves commanded, honoured, and well treated by their own prince. Therefore, it is necessary to prepare yourself with such soldiers as these, so that with Italian virtue,* you will be able to defend yourself against foreigners. Although Swiss and Spanish infantry may be considered terrifying, nevertheless both have defects, so that a third kind of military organization could not only oppose them but also be confident of overcoming them. For the Spanish cannot withstand cavalry, and the Swiss have to fear infantry, when they discover those who are as stubborn in combat as they are. Therefore, it has been seen, and experience will show, that the Spanish cannot withstand French cavalry and that Spanish infantrymen can destroy the Swiss. Although this last weakness has not yet been seen, there was nevertheless a taste of it at the battle of Ravenna,* when the Spanish infantry met the German battalions that employ the same order of battle as the Swiss. Aided by bucklers* and their own agility, the Spanish got in between and underneath the Germans' long pikes and were able to hurt them at their pleasure, without the Germans having any remedy. And had it not been for the cavalry charge that broke them, the Spaniards would have slaughtered them all. Therefore, as the defects of both these kinds of infantry are recognized, a new type can be organized that is able to withstand cavalry and has no fear of foot-soldiers. This will occur with the way the armed forces are created and a change in the order of battle. These are among those matters that, from their novel organization, give reputation and greatness to a new prince.

This opportunity, therefore, must not be allowed to pass by, so that Italy may behold her redeemer after so long a time. Nor can I express with what love he will be received in all those territories that have suffered through these foreign floods; with what thirst for revenge, with what stubborn loyalty, with what devotion, with what tears! What doors will be closed to him? What people will deny him their obedience? What envy could oppose him? What Italian could deny him homage? This barbarian dominion stinks in everyone's nostrils! Therefore, may Your Illustrious House take up this task with the spirit and the hope with which just enterprises are begun, so that under your banner this country may be ennobled, and under your auspices those words of Petrarch may come true:

> Virtue will seize arms
> Against frenzy, and the battle will be brief:
> For ancient valour
> Is not yet dead in Italian hearts.*

EXPLANATORY NOTES

Information on historical figures mentioned in the text will be found in the Glossary of Proper Names.

5 *the Magnificent Lorenzo de' Medici*: not Lorenzo the Magnificent (1449–92) but Lorenzo, Duke of Urbino (1492–1519).

iuniori salutem: no manuscripts of *The Prince* in Machiavelli's hand have survived. The manuscripts upon which contemporary critical editions are based come, therefore, from copies of copies. There is every reason to believe that Machiavelli's autograph manuscript employed Latin chapter titles, and we have retained the original Latin titles in this translation. Chapter numbers, however, were not included in the oldest extant manuscripts of the work and have been added over the centuries by editors and translators when the first editions of *The Prince* were printed in Italian or in translation.

will most please him: the opening lines of Machiavelli's dedication recall the classical oration *To Nicoles* composed by the Greek rhetorician Isocrates. This work was popular among Italian humanists, many of whom owned manuscript copies of it, and Latin translations were published in Italy in 1482 and 1492 that Machiavelli no doubt read. For the rhetorical structure of *The Prince*, see Maurizio Viroli, *Machiavelli* (Oxford: Oxford University Press, 1998).

to their greatness: as Giorgio Inglese notes in his critical edition (*De Principatibus* (Rome: Istituto storico italiano per il medio evo, 1994), 11), a manuscript entitled the *Excerpta Riccardi* reports that Lorenzo was far more pleased by the gift of a pair of hunting dogs than by the manuscript of *The Prince* that Machiavelli presented to him at the same time. This *Excerpta Riccardi* manuscript has been dated around 1580, and therefore the anecdote is probably apocryphal.

a long experience in modern affairs and a continuous study of antiquity: the combination of practical political experience of current affairs and a more erudite study of classical antiquity—its history and its political theory—is what makes Machiavelli's approach to statecraft so original. Though he worked in the Florentine Chancery from 1498 to 1512, often observing many of the key figures discussed in *The Prince* (Louis XII, Cesare Borgia, Pope Alexander VI, Pope Julius II, Pope Leo X, the Emperor Maximilian, and a host of other minor figures), he believed that contemporary events could be explained by reference to the greatest figures from the ancient past. During his second encounter with Cesare Borgia in 1502, for example, he asked his friend Biagio Buonaccorsi to send him a copy of Plutarch's *Lives*. Having under his very eyes the archetypal modern prince, Machiavelli obviously wanted to measure him against the heroes of the past.

5 *the gravity of its contents*: as any reader in Machiavelli's day knew very well, declaring that a work was simple and without rhetorical flourishes also constituted a rhetorical figure with many classical antecedents. Since the work was composed following the rules of classical rhetoric, Machiavelli was not employing unnecessary ornamentation in his writing style *because* he was following the rules.

6 *the greatness that Fortune*: the first appearance of the key concept of *fortuna* in *The Prince*. In this translation the word is capitalized when it refers to the abstract concept of Fortune, the idea Machiavelli personifies as a woman giving her fickle favours only to young men in Chapter XXV. This power was recognized by both classical antiquity and medieval and Renaissance writers as the arbitrary force in human affairs that makes it extremely difficult to predict the outcome of any event. When the word is not capitalized in this translation, it generally refers to a less abstract or philosophical notion and may often simply mean good or bad luck, particularly when the Italian word *fortuna* is modified by an adjective.

I unjustly suffer a great and continuous malignity of Fortune: Machiavelli was exiled from political life in 1512 upon the return of the Medici to power and the overthrow of the republican regime of Piero Soderini (1452–1522), whose regime he had served. During the rest of his life Machiavelli was never really allowed to return to any position of power or authority so long as the Medici controlled the city. In the famous private letter to Francesco Vettori, dated 10 December 1513, describing the composition of *The Prince*, Machiavelli declares that he would even occupy himself by rolling stones if he could find employment with the Medici. He thus implicitly compares himself to Sisyphus, a Greek king condemned to Hades for double-dealing and punished by being forced to roll boulders uphill, only to have them roll down again for eternity. Machiavelli would have found Sisyphus in Ovid's *Metamorphoses* (4. 460). But Machiavelli was also an avid reader of Dante, and he would have also found a reference to Sisyphus in the fourth circle of Hell in Dante's *Inferno*, where the avaricious and the spendthrifts are forced to push boulders endlessly. This Canto 7 is particularly relevant to *The Prince*, since it is here that Virgil describes the classical goddess of Fortune and declares that she is under the control of the Providence of the Christian God. Machiavelli will declare that at least one-half of human actions are controlled by Fortune in Chapter XXV, but nowhere agrees with Dante that Divine Providence controls Fortune. Machiavelli also wrote a *capitolo*, a poetic composition in *terza rima*, about Fortune and dedicated it to Giovan Battista Soderini (1484–1528), the nephew of Pier Soderini, the Gonfaloniere of the Florentine Republic for whom he worked in the city's government.

7 *either republics or principalities*: in this single sentence Machiavelli

employs three important terms relating to political power: *stato* (state), *dominio* (dominion), and *imperio* (power). The terms are closely related, but Machiavelli has no rigid definitions of what they imply. Machiavelli's *stato* is certainly not the nineteenth-century nation state. His use of the term refers to an institutional exercise of power and the territory over which that power is exercised. *Dominio* is less comprehensive, usually referring to the military and political control over a territory. *Imperio* alludes to sovereignty or territorial control and may be exercised over a *stato*.

or they are new: the traditional Latin treatises on the ideal prince and his education (known as the *specula principis* or 'mirror-for-princes' literature) invariably focused upon rulers with hereditary rights to power. Machiavelli's originality derives from his interest in the 'new' rulers, upstarts without traditional bloodlines but with ability, courage, and good luck, as well as his subversive critique of the main principles of conventional doctrines about the good prince.

as was Milan for Francesco Sforza: after serving the Visconti rulers of Milan and then the city's Ambrosian Republic against Venice, Sforza struck a deal with the Venetians in 1448 and seized control of Milan in 1450.

for the King of Spain: on 11 November 1500, in the secret Treaty of Granada, King Ferdinand of Spain agreed with King Louis XII of France to divide the Kingdom of Naples, then ruled by Ferdinand's cousin, King Frederick I of Aragon.

either through Fortune or through virtue: here two of the most important concepts in *The Prince*—*fortuna* and *virtù*—are linked for the first time (see also Chapters VI–IX). *Virtù* is related to the Latin *virtus* and *vir*, and is a decidedly masculine quality, denoting ingenuity, skill, and ability. It can rarely be rendered accurately by references to our present-day association of the word with moral 'virtue'. Like *stato*, *fortuna*, *ordini*, and a number of Machiavelli's favourite terms, there is no single and automatic meaning for the term *virtù*. Here it is rendered as 'virtue', but the reader can detect from the context the correct nuance.

at length elsewhere: this remark has led many scholars to assume that the *Discourses on Livy* was begun before *The Prince*, since Book I of the *Discourses on Livy* deals with the same topic. However, it is also possible that this sentence was merely added to *The Prince* after it was completed, during the composition of the *Discourses on Livy*. Had Machiavelli revised his manuscript for publication such textual questions would be far easier to answer, but since both *The Prince* and the *Discourses on Livy* were posthumously published they are probably incapable of ever being resolved conclusively.

8 *the Duke of Ferrara*: Machiavelli actually refers to two different dukes: Ercole I fought the Salt War against Venice and managed to remain in

power, but lost territory in a treaty signed in 1484; Alfonso I (Ercole's son) was attacked in 1510 by the Holy League, organized by Pope Julius II, who also excommunicated Alfonso; but like his father, Alfonso retained his hold over Ferrara. The Este family had controlled Ferrara and its surrounding territory since around 1240, and would remain a powerful force in that city until the Napoleonic period.

8 *indentations for the construction of another*: here Machiavelli employs a technical term from architecture—*addentellato*—the dovetailed or tooth-like projections of masonry on the top or ends of walls that enable new masonry to be fitted tightly and firmly onto the older structure without slipping. Implicit in this metaphor is the concept of the state as a work of art, shaped by the architect-like ruler into the proper form he desires.

strong medicines: another famous Machiavellian metaphor, implicit in his belief that the able ruler may be compared to a skilled physician who diagnoses illnesses before they have gone beyond the possibility of any cure.

9 *just as quickly lost it*: King Louis XII took Milan in February 1499, driving Ludovico Sforza into exile in Germany, but Sforza returned a year later on 5 February 1500, only to be betrayed by his Swiss troops at the battle of Novara, where he was captured on 5 April 1500.

if only a Duke Ludovico: Machiavelli's use of the indefinite article 'a' expresses his contempt for this ruler's ineptitude.

the whole world: in 1511 Pope Julius II organized the Holy League to drive Louis XII and the French out of Italy. The League's members included most of the other European powers (hence, Machiavelli's characterization of it as 'the whole world')—not only Spain, Venice, and the Papal States but also (at least on paper) the England of Henry VIII and the Germany of Emperor Maximilian I. In April 1512 Louis XII won a pyrrhic victory over League forces at Ravenna, but was forced to withdraw from the peninsula.

and Normandy: Normandy was annexed to France in 1204; Gascony was taken back from the English in 1453; Burgundy was joined to France in 1477; and Brittany was added to the Kingdom of France in 1491 through the marriage of King Charles VIII to Anne of Brittany, who subsequently married King Louis XII.

10 *the Turk in Greece*: Machiavelli generally refers to the Ottoman Empire and its ruler with a collective singular noun—'the Turk'. By Greece he means the entire Balkan Peninsula, not the present European state. The Ottoman Turks crossed the Hellespont as early as 1354, and in 1453 Mohammed II conquered Constantinople, destroying the last vestiges of the ancient Byzantine Empire, a Christian state. The conquest of the Greek peninsula by the Turks was not completed until 1461.

shackles: Machiavelli employs the Latin term *compedes*—shackles or fetters.

11 *when the Aetolians brought the Romans into Greece*: in 211 BC the Romans supported a coalition of Greeks against Phillip V of Macedon. This Aetolian League opposed the Achaean League, allied with Macedon. The first war with Phillip V was won by him, and it was only in a second war, terminating in the Roman victory at the battle of Cynoscephalae (197 BC), that the Romans and their Greek allies defeated Macedon. But during the second war the Aetolian League shifted alliances and became the allies of Antiochus III of Syria against the Romans, while the Achaean League, once allied with Phillip V, now changed sides and supported Rome in the successful victory over Phillip V. The shifting alliances and frequent wars of classical antiquity were just as complex as the similar changes of alliances between Italian and European states in Italy during the fifteenth and sixteenth centuries.

12 *they put down the Kingdom of Macedon*: by their victory at Cynoscephalae (197 BC).

Antiochus was driven out: after defeats by Rome and her allies at the battles of Thermopylae (191 BC) and Magnesia (190 BC).

consumptive illnesses: Machiavelli refers to a severe form of tuberculosis in this famous metaphor of the ruler as physician and political crises as illnesses requiring quick diagnosis for a cure.

13 *of Louis and not of Charles*: Louis XII, not Charles VIII. Louis retained power in Italy from 1499 to 1513, while Charles exercised power in Italy between 1494 and 1495.

because of the ambition of the Venetians: in the Treaty of Blois (15 April 1499) France promised Venice Cremona and the Ghiara d'Adda in return for support against the Duchy of Milan.

because of the actions of King Charles: Charles's invasion of Italy provoked the eventual alliance of Venice, Milan, Florence, Naples, Mantua, the Empire, and Spain against France. Their combined forces met Charles's army at the battle of Fornovo (1495), but they missed the opportunity to destroy the French army, allowing Charles to escape.

Genoa surrendered: on 26 October 1499.

the Florentines became his allies: in October 1499 Florence allied herself with Charles VIII in return for assistance in a campaign to conquer Pisa.

all rushed to become his ally: respectively, Gian Francesco Gonzaga of Mantua; Ercole I d'Este of Ferrara; Giovanni II Bentivoglio of Bologna; Caterina Sforza Riario, the Countess of Forlì; Astorre III Manfredi (1485–1502) of Faenza; Pandolfo V Malatesta of Rimini (1475–1534); Giovanni Sforza (1466–1510) of Pesaro; Giulio Cesare da Verano (1432–1502) of Camerino; and Jacopo IV d'Appiano (1460–1510) of Piombino.

two-thirds of Italy: some manuscripts read 'one-third of Italy', a figure that seems closer to the truth. But Machiavelli apparently meant to include the Kingdom of Naples in this calculation, since it was technically a tributary to the Kingdom of France. If this is the case, two-thirds is closer to the mark.

14 *obliged to continue*: after supporting Pope Alexander VI and Cesare Borgia in the taking of Imola and Forlì, Louis XII was forced to agree to the capture of Pesaro, Rimini, Faenza, and Piombino.

to keep him from becoming the ruler of Tuscany: the Valdichiana region and the city of Arezzo rebelled against their Florentine rulers in June 1502, and it seemed that Cesare Borgia intended to attack the city of Florence as well. But since Florence was the traditional ally of France, Louis XII forced Borgia to back down: Arezzo was recaptured and eventually returned to Florentine control on 26 August 1502.

Louis replaced him: after driving out King Frederick I of Aragon, Ferdinand II of Aragon and V of Castile and Leon shared control of the Kingdom of Naples with his temporary ally King Louis, but Ferdinand was far cleverer than the King of France and eventually took complete control of the kingdom away from the French.

reducing the dominion of the Venetians: supposedly aimed against the Ottoman Turks, the League of Cambrai (10 December 1508)—formed by Louis XII, Pope Julius II, Ferdinand of Spain, the Emperor Maximilian I, and a number of minor figures—actually targeted the Republic of Venice and her possessions on the Italian mainland. Venice was excommunicated by the Pope and the French defeated her ground forces at the disastrous battle of Agnadello (also known as Vailà) on 14 May 1509.

15 *the cardinal's hat for the Archbishop of Rouen*: in return for a dispensation allowing Louis XII to divorce his wife Jeanne and to marry Anne of Brittany (the widow of Charles VIII), as well as the promotion of Georges d'Amboise, Archbishop of Rouen, to the rank of cardinal, Louis XII agreed to help Pope Alexander VI in his plans to regain territory in the Romagna, employing his son Cesare Borgia as his military commander. Cesare Borgia himself carried out the negotiations between the Pope and the King, personally carrying with him to France the papal bull with the annulment in December 1498. The marriage between Louis and Anne quickly took place shortly thereafter in January 1499.

what I shall say later about the promises of princes and how they should be observed: see Chapter XVIII.

at Nantes: Machiavelli met Georges d'Amboise at Nantes between 25 October and 4 November 1500, when he represented the Republic of Florence on a diplomatic mission to the French court.

Valentino (as Cesare Borgia, son of Pope Alexander, was commonly called): in August 1498, after abandoning his titles as Archbishop of Valencia and cardinal (both offices he received from his father, Pope Alexander VI), Cesare Borgia received the title Duke of Valentois from King Louis XII, a reward to entice the Pope into agreeing to the annulment of the King's marriage with his first wife and his remarriage to the wife of Charles VIII.

16 *Alexander's successors*: seven of Alexander the Great's best generals divided up his empire that stretched from Greece to Egypt, Syria, and Persia.

17 *sanjaks*: Machiavelli employs an Italian version (*sangiachie*) of the Turkish word, meaning an administrative district of a Turkish vilayet or province.

19 *creating an oligarchy there that will keep the state friendly toward you*: Machiavelli's term for oligarchy is *uno stato di pochi*.

by establishing oligarchies there: after the end of the Peloponnesian War (431–404 BC) the victorious Spartans tore down the city walls defending Athens and established a government favourable to them known as the Thirty Tyrants, but a democratic government hostile to Sparta was re-established after 403 BC. After defeating the Thebans in 382 BC, the Spartans established a pro-Spartan oligarchy in the city that lasted three years, but through the efforts of Pelopidas and Epaminondas this oligarchy was eventually overthrown as well.

and did not lose them: Capua was punished (not completely destroyed) in 211 BC for its support of Hannibal in the Second Punic War (218–201 BC) after Rome recaptured the city. Carthage was destroyed at the end of the Third Punic War (149–146 BC) by Scipio Aemilianus in 146 BC. Numantia in Spain was destroyed by the same general in 133 BC.

in order to retain it: even though Titus Quinctius Flaminius, the conquering Roman general who defeated Phillip V of Macedon at the battle of Cynoscephalae (197 BC), declared the independence of the Greek city-states in 196 BC, after a number of wars and uprisings against Roman influence, the Romans destroyed Greek independence after the battle of Leucopetra in 146 BC. After that date Greece effectively became a province of Rome, and in the process, Corinth, Thebes, and Euboea were badly damaged.

20 *just as Pisa did*: Florence purchased Pisa in 1405 from Gabriele Visconti and occupied the city in the following year, but the Pisans rebelled against Florentine control in 1494 when Charles VIII invaded Italy. Pisa was retaken by the Florentine republic only in 1509, during a military campaign in which Machiavelli played a political role.

proceed in their affairs by imitation: like many Renaissance thinkers, Machiavelli believed that history could instruct his contemporaries and that modern practice should follow the best procedures of the ancient world (almost always those of republican Rome).

do as those prudent archers do: like Machiavelli, Baldesar Castiglione's *The Book of the Courtier* (1528)—the only Italian book to rival the audience of *The Prince* during the European Renaissance—employs the metaphor of the archer in discussing the doctrine of imitation: 'and if, for all that, they are unable to attain to that perfection, such as it is, that I have tried to express, the one who comes the nearest to it will be the most perfect; as when many archers shoot at a target and none of them hits the bull's eye, the one who comes closest is surely better than all the rest' (*The Book of the Courtier*, trans. Charles Singleton (New York: Norton, 2002), 7).

21 *and others of their kind*: it should be noted that Machiavelli mixes historical and literary figures somewhat indiscriminately here from his readings of the Old Testament, Livy, Plutarch, and Xenophon.

   the material they could mould into whatever form they liked: Machiavelli's metaphors describing the ideal prince's actions suggest an artistic quality to political action, by comparing the prince to an artist fashioning a work of art from a shapeless mass of inchoate material.

22 *that opportunity*: the Machiavellian formula for success requires a convergence of three qualities: *virtù* (virtue in the non-moral sense, implying ability, ingenuity, or skill); *fortuna* (Fortune, that is, the favour of the fickle classical goddess personified in Chapter XXV of *The Prince* as a woman, and not merely temporary good luck); and *occasione* (the opportunity, recognized only by the quality of *virtù*).

   the new institutions and methods: two other important terms in Machiavelli's often vague political vocabulary: *ordini* (institutions, laws, regulations) and *modi* (methods, procedures). The term *ordini* is particularly important in the *Discourses on Livy*, where the *virtù* of a single heroic figure is less important than how that hero's ability or skill in creating a state can be institutionalized in a long-lasting republican form of government. But in the *Discourses on Livy* the exceptional *virtù* of heroic figures is quite important for the foundation and for the redemption of republics and principalities. Instituting new *ordini e modi*, for Machiavelli, is the most difficult task of the statesman.

   Brother Girolamo Savonarola: Machiavelli sometimes showed little sympathy for Savonarola, even though the friar's plan to institute a Grand Council of some 3,600 citizens in Florence would have been an extension of republican participation in the state's affairs. In a private letter to Ricciardo Becchi dated 8 March 1498, Machiavelli described one of Savonarola's impassioned sermons quite critically. However, he later also spoke of Savonarola with great respect in his discussion of politics and religion in the *Discourses on Livy* (1. 11).

23 *lacked nothing to reign but a kingdom*: Machiavelli's source is the *History* (22. 4) of Justin, a second- or third-century AD historian who wrote a Latin epitome (a summary or abridgement) of the *Historiae Philippicae* or *Philippic Histories* by Pompeius Trogus, a contemporary of Livy. Trogus' history in forty-four books focused upon the history of Macedon and suggested that the empires of the Parthians or the Macedonians were equally as important as that of Rome. As is frequently the case, Machiavelli's citations in Latin are slightly different from the Latin texts

contemporary readers use today, since he employed manuscripts or editions different from our modern critical editions. Some scholars detect the influence of Polybius (7. 8) here as well. Machiavelli says something similar about Walter, the Duke of Athens, a would-be tyrant of Florence expelled from the city in 1343 in his *Florentine Histories* (2. 34): 'nor did he lack anything as prince but the title' (*Florentine Histories*, trans. Laura F. Banfield and Harvey Mansfield (Princeton: Princeton University Press, 1988), 91).

25 *having conquered the Romagna*: Borgia took Imola on 27 November 1499 (its citadel fell on 11 December 1499); Forlì on 19 December 1499 (its citadel fell on 12 January 1500); Cesena on 2 August 1500; Rimini on 10 October 1500; Pesaro on 21 October 1500; and Faenza after a long siege on 25 April 1501. The political reality in the Romagna was that the papal authority was only nominal, since most of the cities there that supposedly owed allegiance to the Papal States were ruled by local princes or tyrants.

beaten down the Colonna: the Colonna family backed the deposed King of Naples, Frederick I of Aragon, and when the forces of France and Spain deposed Frederick, the Colonna fell out of power in Rome and were subsequently excommunicated by Pope Alexander VI, who also confiscated a number of their fortresses.

26 *when the Duke invaded Tuscany*: Borgia's troops made an incursion into Tuscan territory after his attack on Bologna in 1501, but there was probably never any threat to Florence herself. On 7 June 1502, Vitellozzo Vitelli, a mercenary soldier serving under Borgia's orders, captured the city of Arezzo, but by August he had withdrawn from the city.

the capture of the Duchy of Urbino: Urbino fell on 20 July 1502, and Borgia forced its ruler, Guido Baldo da Montefeltro, into exile in Venice. Camerino surrendered to Borgia on 20 July as well, and its ruler, Giulio Cesare da Varano, was taken prisoner and subsequently killed.

a meeting at Magione: on 24 September 1502, a number of Borgia's enemies met at the small town of Magione near Perugia: they included Paulo Orsini, Francesco Orsini (Duke of Gravina), Cardinal Giambattista Orsini, Vitellozzo Vitelli, Oliverotto of Fermo, Giampaolo Baglioni of Perugia, and representatives from Urbino and Siena.

countless dangers for the Duke: shortly after the Magione meeting, Guido Baldo returned to Urbino, Giovanni Maria, Giulio Cesare da Varano's son, returned to Camerino, and both Imola and Rimini were threatened by troops hostile to Borgia.

reconciled themselves with him: in Imola on 29 October 1502 Paulo Orsini signed an agreement with Borgia that confirmed his earlier military contract with the Duke.

and into his clutches: the stupidity of the Orsini in believing such a shrewd liar as Cesare Borgia is even more remarkable in that Paulo Orsini and Vitellozzo Vitelli conquered Senigallia for Borgia, ousting Francesco

Maria della Rovere from power there, before Borgia arrived and had them arrested for their troubles, along with Oliverotto of Fermo and the Duke of Gravina, on 31 December 1502.

26 *Having wiped out these leaders*: Vitellozzo Vitelli and Oliverotto of Fermo were strangled on the very night of their arrest on 31 December 1503. After Borgia's father the Pope had captured other Orsini leaders, the two Orsini captured (Paulo and the Duke of Gravina) were strangled on 18 January 1503. For a dramatic account of Borgia's suppression of his enemies, see Machiavelli's *A Description of the Methods Used by Duke Valentino in Killing Vitellozzo Vitelli, Oliverotto da Fermo, and Others*, in Allen Gilbert (ed. and trans.), *Chief Works of Machiavelli*, 3 vols. (Durham, NC: Duke University Press, 1965), i. 163–9. This earlier treatment, based on personal experience as a Florentine diplomat, serves as the basis for what Machiavelli included in *The Prince*.

27 *a very distinguished president*: Antonio Ciocchi di Monte San Savino (d. 1533), who later became Bishop of Città di Castello in 1503 and then Cardinal in 1511. His tribunal included representatives from the major cities of the Romagna (Cesena, Rimini, Forlì, Pesaro, Fano, Faenza, and Imola).

satisfied and stupefied at the same time: named governor of the Romagna in 1501, Remirro may also have been suspected of financial improprieties and even dealings with the conspirators at Magione. Whatever his offence (if there were one), Borgia did not hesitate to sacrifice his lieutenant on 26 December 1502, in a bloody execution that some contemporary scholars have interpreted as a kind of theatrical spectacle with a political message. Some of Machiavelli's diplomatic correspondence with the Republic of Florence discusses this event.

28 *against the Spaniards besieging Gaeta*: after the French and Spanish quarrelled over the spoils from capturing the Kingdom of Naples, the French suffered several military defeats and abandoned Gaeta and Naples on 2 January 1504.

very few saved themselves: Borgia had Astorre Manfredi of Faenza killed on 2 June 1502; Giulio Cesare da Verano and three of his sons were murdered after Camerino fell; but some of their relatives survived, and those he was unable to capture and murder returned immediately after receiving the news of the illness and death of Pope Alexander VI.

a large faction in the College of Cardinals: Borgia thought he could rely on the votes of the eleven Spanish cardinals (there were thirty-eight cardinals in all).

Perugia and Piombino: in January 1503 Perugia was taken; in September 1501, Piombino was captured.

Pisa under his protection: an agreement to this effect had been drawn up and signed on 8 August 1503, in Rome.

Alexander died: on 18 August 1503.

29 *all the others up in the air*: actually the rulers of Urbino, Città di Castello, Perugia, and Piombino managed to return almost immediately after September 1503.

enemy armies: while the election of a new pope took place, a Spanish army occupied Naples and the French forces stood near Rome, with Borgia between them.

more than a month for him: some fortresses held by Borgia in the Romagna did not surrender until the end of 1503 and others even resisted until August 1504. Several were surrendered in return for the safe-conduct pass given to Borgia when he left Rome and went to Naples.

he was safe: an exaggeration, since Borgia basically lived at the mercy of his French protectors and the new Pope, who soon proved to be Borgia's enemy, even though Spanish support for his election to the papacy had been crucial.

he himself said to me: Machiavelli spoke personally to Borgia while he was on a diplomatic mission for the Republic of Florence in Rome during the papal election (26 October–18 December 1503). At that time Giuliano della Rovere was elected to the papacy as Julius II as a result of a compromise between the French and Spanish cardinals.

30 *to someone he did not like*: Machiavelli completely ignores the fact that, after the death of Pope Alexander VI, another man (Francesco Todeschini Piccolomini, 1439–1503) succeeded Cesare Borgia's father Alexander VI as Pius III from 22 September to 18 October 1503. Pius III had been elected precisely because he was ill and would probably not live long, and thus his election guaranteed a brief reign while the two most important factions in the College of Cardinals, Spain and France, could come to some agreement on a real choice. Actually, Machiavelli should probably have considered the election of Pius III as at least a temporary victory for Cesare Borgia.

and Cardinal Ascanio: this list of anti-Borgia cardinals includes some by name and others by the name of the church to which their titles were connected. They are respectively Giuliano della Rovere (St Peter's in Chains); Cardinal Giovanni Colonna; Raffaele Riario (San Giorgio); Cardinal Ascanio Sforza. Except for the Cardinal of Rouen, Georges d'Amboise, each of these individuals had reason to hate Borgia for injuries done to him or his family.

the cause of his ultimate ruin: Borgia promised Giuliano della Rovere (Pope Julius II) the support of the Spanish cardinals in the papal election in return for naming him Gonfaloniere (Standard-bearer) of the Church, a military position that he felt might help him retain his hold on the Romagna. At first Julius may have thought that Borgia could be used against his enemies the Venetians, but if that were the case he soon changed his mind and had Borgia arrested at the end of November 1503.

Borgia traded his last strongholds in the Romagna for a safe-conduct pass to Naples, where he arrived on 28 April 1504, only to be arrested by the Spanish Viceroy, Gonzalo Ferandez de Còrdoba. Obviously the Spanish had also made some deal with Julius. Borgia was sent under guard to Spain on 2 August 1504, where he was imprisoned. Escaping in 1506, Borgia went to serve the King of Navarre as a military leader and was killed on 12 March 1506 in an insignificant skirmish. Machiavelli's exemplary military and political leader was only 32 when he died.

30 *in a treatise on republics*: some scholars use this remark to argue for a dating of the *Discourses on Livy* as subsequent to 1513 and the composition of *The Prince*. Others have argued that the *Discourses on Livy* was begun first but was interrupted by Machiavelli to write *The Prince* because of the particular historical and political situation that existed at that date (a Medici pope, Leo X, in Rome, and Medici family members controlling the city of Florence at the same time).

his native city: the word *patria* is almost always associated by Machiavelli in his works with a city-state, not a 'country' in our contemporary sense of the word. However, the word *patria* also implies a very strong moral and political pathos in Machiavelli's vocabulary, even if translating the word as 'fatherland' conjures up rather sinister connotations. In a letter to Francesco Vettori dated 16 April 1527 Machiavelli declares that he loves his *patria* more than his soul.

31 *leaving Sicily to Agathocles*: Machiavelli's treatment of Agathocles seems to have come from Justin's epitome of Pompeius Trogus (see n. to p. 23), but Diodorus Siculus and Polybius also mention him. Actually the western portion of Sicily remained under Carthaginian control.

acquire power but not glory: in this important statement, Machiavelli separates *virtù* from the completely immoral actions of Agathocles, declaring that such misdeeds can only earn *dominio* (power) but not glory. Yet he has just completed the praise of Cesare Borgia, whose deeds included all of the kinds of evil actions typical of Agathocles. One explanation is that Machiavelli considered Borgia's cruelties necessary, whereas those of Agathocles were senselessly cruel and unnecessary. Another possible explanation for this apparent contradiction is that Machiavelli excused some evil means if the end was sufficiently noble. In the case of Borgia, Machiavelli felt that with the combination of papal power (Alexander VI) and Borgia's military prowess, a strong, central Italian state might be established that could protect Italy from foreign invasions. Subsequently, in 1513 when he composed *The Prince*, a similar situation existed, with a Medici pope in power and Medici princes (first Giuliano, Duke of Nemours, then Lorenzo, Duke of Urbino) in control of the city of Florence. Florence and a Medici pope might also form the nucleus of a central Italian state that could guarantee Italian independence. When this opportunity disappeared with the death of Leo X and that of Lorenzo, Duke of Urbino, by 1519, the practical goal of *The Prince* disappeared, probably explaining why Machiavelli did not publish the work during his lifetime.

32 *after Paulo died*: on 1 October 1499, executed by his Florentine employers.

a magnificent solemn banquet: on 26 December 1501.

33 *killed Giovanni and all the others*: since Fermo was then a free republic, Oliverotto was actually establishing a tyrannical government, not merely replacing another tyrant. Thus, it would have been sensible for him to remove any citizen with enough influence, power, or wealth to oppose his designs.

his parricide: strictly speaking, Giovanni Fogliani was Oliverotto's uncle, not his father, but he did serve as Oliverotto's father when the boy was young.

whether cruelty be badly or well used: Machiavelli's entire discussion of cruelty focuses upon the practical and technical results of a cruel action, not its moral or ethical significance. But even for those readers of Machiavelli who believe him to be amoral or immoral, the sarcastic phrase 'if it is permitted to speak well of evil' implicitly admits that there is a moral realm where such cruel actions may be condemned.

35 *two different humours*: Renaissance medical theory (inherited from classical medical treatises and the practice of Hippocrates and Galen) held that the human body was governed by four different 'humours': blood, black bile, yellow bile, and phlegm. In like manner, the body politic mimicked the human body in being dominated by various kinds of similar forces.

37 *citizens and subjects*: Machiavelli generally distinguishes between the members of a city-state who have rights and privileges and participate in the municipal government, on the one hand, and those people who live in the surrounding *dominio* (territory or dominion), and who have fewer, if any, rights of the citizen. Here he notes that even in a government controlled by a prince there can be active participation in the government by its citizens—what Machiavelli calls an *ordine civile* ('proper civil society')—without that government necessarily evolving into an absolute form.

38 *The first case has already been treated*: in Chapters VI–VII (and subsequently in Chapters XII–XIII).

40 *the act of a presumptuous and foolhardy man to do so*: again, when Machiavelli discusses the Church there is a note of sarcasm (and presumably the implicit assertion that he, a presumptuous and foolhardy man, indeed intends to discuss this topic).

41 *should seize more territory*: Machiavelli's original phrase, to seize 'più stato', is an excellent example of why his political vocabulary is flexible and must be translated according to its context. Here, the context obviously demands 'more territory', not 'more state'.

41 *in the defence of Ferrara*: in 1482 Ercole I of Ferrara, supported by Milan and Florence, went to war with Venice; the war ended in 1484 with Ferrara's autonomy preserved at the cost of the loss of some territory to Venice.

Pope Sixtus: Pope Sixtus IV.

by a method never before used by Alexander or his predecessors: this is a puzzling remark, since all Renaissance popes, and especially Alexander VI and Julius II, were simonists and sold church offices to a scandalous degree. Perhaps Machiavelli refers to the sale of indulgences, a practice that is usually identified with the papacy of Leo X (1475–1521), and one that enraged Martin Luther and religious reformers in northern Europe.

42 *His Holiness Pope Leo*: Pope Leo X.

his countless virtues: one of the few times in *The Prince* when the context of the word *virtù* seems to include this moral connotation and not the more technical and political connotations of ingenuity, ability, or skill.

43 *the invasion of the foreigner came*: that of King Charles VIII of France in 1494–5.

take Italy with a piece of chalk: in his *Mémoires* (7. 4), the French historian Philippe de Commynes reports that the French army marked the houses in which they quartered their troops with chalk. The contemptuous tone of Machiavelli's phrase underscores his belief that Italian resistance to Charles was virtually non-existent.

spoke the truth: the man in question is no doubt Brother Girolamo Savonarola, whose sermon of 1 November 1494 interpreted the successful French invasion as a divinely sent castigation of the sins of Italy, the Church, and Florence.

44 *at Caravaggio*: 14 September 1488.

Sforza, his father: Muzio Attendolo Sforza.

45 *at Vailà*: at this battle, also known as Agnadello (14 May 1509), Venice was soundly defeated by French troops.

in a single day: since the technical term for a day's battle is 'una giornata' in the vocabulary of Machiavelli's day, his phrase could also be translated as 'in a single battle'. In the case of this battle, the combat did only last a single day.

eight hundred years of exhausting effort to acquire: this is a gross exaggeration, since Venice lost none of her extremely valuable overseas territories on which her commercial empire was really based. Venetian conquest of mainland territory had slowly taken place since the fourteenth century. Machiavelli must mean that in what he considers the eight-hundred-year history of Venice, this was the republic's worst military disaster.

46 *these 'condottieri' have conducted Italy into slavery and disgrace*: Machiavelli here puns on the meaning of the word *condotta*, which is not only the past participle of the verb *condurre* (to conduct), but also, as a noun

(*la condotta*), can refer to the contract by which a mercenary soldier is engaged by his employer. The term *condotta* also explains the origin of the Italian term for such soldiers: *condottieri*—soldiers with a *condotta* or contract who fight for money.

47 *and his armies*: when Julius II attempted to conquer Ferrara, through the formation of the Holy League in 1511, Ferdinand I of Aragon promised to assist him.

at Ravenna: on 11 April 1512.

to take Pisa: in June 1500 France sent a group of Swiss and French troops to assist Florence.

the Emperor of Constantinople: John VI Cantacuzene. In his wars against the rightful Byzantine heir, John Palaeologus (1347–55), this ruler brought in Ottoman troops to assist him. As a result of this, the Turks gained a foothold in Europe for the first time, eventually destroying the Byzantine Empire in the following century by the capture of Constantinople in 1453.

48 *he captured Imola and Forlì*: between November 1499 and January 1500.

49 *a figure from the Old Testament*: Machiavelli specifically calls David a *figura*, not an *exemplo* (exemplum). The term comes from biblical exegesis, and underlines the fact that the individual involved is a true historical figure (not an abstract allegory) who also may have symbolic dimensions. The greatest example of figural representation in Italian literature is Dante's *Divine Comedy*, a work Machiavelli knew very well. Machiavelli's source for the David and Saul story is 1 Samuel 17: 38–40. The biblical account of the death of Goliath reports that David had a staff and a slingshot and that Goliath was decapitated by his own sword. The story became one of republican Florence's most famous myths, with David representing the embattled republican government and Goliath its more imposing enemies. Machiavelli could have seen David represented with a sword in two of the three famous statues in Florence, those by Donatello and Verrocchio. Michelangelo's David carries only his sling. All three of these works were executed and displayed in Florence before Machiavelli wrote *The Prince*.

freed France from the English: at the end of the Hundred Years War (1337–1453).

in his kingdom: Charles VII, who ruled France from 1422 to 1461, organized independent troops of horsemen and infantry, allowing him to free himself from dependence upon soldiers provided by his nobles.

to hire Swiss troops: Louis XII began doing this in 1474.

the Goths as mercenaries: in AD 376 the Emperor Valens began to hire Visigothic troops; Theodosius continued this policy in 382.

50 *non sua vi nixa*: Tacitus, *Annals*, 13. 19.

by those four men: Cesare Borgia, Hiero, David, and Charles VII. It is less likely that, as some have suggested, Machiavelli refers here to the four men of Chapter VI (Moses, Cyrus, Romulus, and Theseus).

50 *Philip, father of Alexander the Great*: Philip II of Macedon.

the only art: the word Machiavelli employs in this paragraph several times to refer to the military profession is *arte*. In Machiavelli's day the word was far closer to 'trade' and 'profession', and in fact *arte* was the word for guild. But Machiavelli explicitly rejects the idea that the military should be a professional force, and therefore the word has been translated as 'art', a translation that is also in keeping with the English title of Machiavelli's analysis of warfare, *L'arte della guerra*—by tradition rendered as *The Art of War*.

Since his sons: Francesco Sforza's three sons were Galeazzo Maria (d. 1476), Ludovico, and Ascanio. Only Ludovico became the ruler of Milan.

52 *backed it up with reasons*: Machiavelli's sources are Plutarch's *Life of Philopomen* and Livy, 35. 28.

and Scipio imitated Cyrus: Machiavelli's sources for these remarks are respectively Plutarch's *Life of Alexander*, 8; Q. Curtius' *History of Alexander the Great*, 4 and 8; Suetonius, *Divus Iulius*, 7; and Cicero's letter *Ad Quintum fratrem*, 1. 8.

the life of Cyrus written by Xenophon: the *Cyropaedia*, the title of which means 'the education of Cyrus'.

in purity: one of the popular themes in Italian Renaissance painting—the continence of Scipio—was inspired by the story of how Scipio returned unharmed to her fiancé a woman who had been taken during the capture of the Spanish city of New Carthage. Normally, soldiers taking a city would loot, pillage, rape, and burn. The source of this tale is Livy, 26. 50, and Petrarch's Latin epic based on Livy, *Africa*, 4. 375–88.

53 *many have written about this*: the traditional advice-to-princes literature has a long history, stretching back to the classical antecedents of Plato, Aristotle, Cicero, and Xenophon, to medieval and Renaissance writers such as Dante, Aquinas, Marsilius of Padua, Egidio Colonna, Poggio Bracciolini, Giovanni Pontano, and Erasmus. The Latin chapter titles of *The Prince* often repeat some of the themes of this literature. Chapter XVII, for example, discusses a question often treated in other treatises on the ideal prince. Before Machiavelli, political theorists had argued that it was better to be loved than to be feared. Machiavelli, of course, argues the contrary.

54 *appears to be a virtue*: this is an instance of Machiavelli's use of the term *virtù* where the translation must reflect its traditional moral value, since the context of the word, here coupled with vice, demands such a meaning.

if it is employed virtuously: here the word *virtù* is used as an adverb, but it continues to retain the traditional moral connotation mentioned in the previous note.

55 *to gain the papacy*: attributing Giuliano della Rovere's expenditure in his campaign to become Pope Julius II to generosity rather than simony is to take a generous view of this fascinating individual, obviously admired by Machiavelli for his resolution and bravery.

The present King of France: King Louis XII. Since he died on 31 December 1514, some scholars cite this sentence to argue that Machiavelli did not revise *The Prince* after this date.

the present King of Spain: Ferdinand I of Aragon and V of Castile and Leon.

56 *he would have destroyed the power he acquired*: Machiavelli's sources for the life of Julius Caesar are Cicero's *De Officiis* (1. 14) and Suetonius' *Divus Iulius* (11–12).

57 *brought order to the Romagna*: the verb Machiavelli employs here is *racconciare*—meaning literally to mend or to repair.

to avoid being considered cruel: Pistoia was a Tuscan city subjugated to the Republic of Florence. It was torn by political strife between factions identified with the Panciatichi and the Cancellieri families. Machiavelli was sent there four times in 1501 by the Florentine government to deal with these political upheavals.

fines custode tueri: Virgil, *Aeneid*, 1. 563–4.

59 *his good and bad luck*: it is clear from the context of this statement that by *fortuna* Machiavelli refers here not to the more philosophical concept of Fortune but to common-sense ideas of good and bad luck.

by one of his legates: in 205 BC Quintius Pleminius took Locri (a Greek city in Calabria) back from Hannibal and pillaged it. He was eventually arrested after the Locrians complained to the Roman Senate about his behaviour, but Scipio, under whose command the man served, did nothing to stop him or to punish him. Machiavelli's source is Livy, 29. 8–9.

such a character: Machiavelli provides another comparison of the qualities of Hannibal and Scipio in *Discourses on Livy* (3. 21). His source is again Livy (28–9). Polybius' *Histories* (11. 19) also makes a similar comparison, but there is some question about whether Machiavelli had access to his work.

60 *the other with force*: Machiavelli's source is Cicero, *De Officiis* (1. 11).

This can only mean: Machiavelli's sources are Ovid's *Fasti* (5. 385–6) and Statius' *Achilleid* (2. 381–452). Chiron is also mentioned as the mentor of Achilles in Dante's *Inferno* (12. 71). Machiavelli emphasizes the dual nature of the centaur, wishing to buttress his argument that political action demands both bestial deeds and those more in keeping with humanity. Chiron was a centaur renowned for his wisdom, but other centaurs were famous for their lustfulness. In fact, one of the most famous episodes in classical mythology (and subsequent figurations in both classical and Renaissance or baroque art) was the battle between the Lapiths and the centaurs, who arrived to celebrate a wedding and misbehaved badly until they were driven away by Theseus and others. The theme usually symbolized the triumph of civilization over barbarism. Machiavelli intends to promote political action that admits both civilized and barbaric deeds.

60 *the fox and the lion*: Machiavelli found the reference to these two political symbols in Cicero, *De Officiis* (1. 13). However, Cicero maintains that force and treachery are inhuman and contemptible.

61 *to colour over his failure to keep his word*: in this chapter Machiavelli employs the verb 'to colour' to indicate disguising the truth. A contemporary equivalent might be 'whitewash'.

62 *one must consider the final result*: in spite of some English translations to the contrary, Machiavelli never said that 'the ends justify the means'. Here he simply says that ends ('the final result') matter when no other independent means of establishing a decision exist, 'no tribunal to which to appeal'. He believes that in political affairs there is rarely any such tribunal. In the *Discourses on Livy* (1. 9) there is another important discussion of the relationship of means and ends: 'It is truly appropriate that while the act accuses him, the result excuses him, and when the result is good, like that of Romulus, it will always excuse him, because one should reproach a man who is violent in order to ruin things, not one who is so in order to set them aright' (*Discourses on Livy*, trans. Julia and Peter Bondanella (Oxford: Oxford University Press, 2003), 45). Machiavelli seems willing to excuse some shocking acts (such as the murder of Remus by Romulus) if the deed is done for an extremely important and moral cause (in this case, the foundation of the city of Rome, and implicitly its empire). To justify such an action as the killing of a brother means to render such an action just, and Machiavelli certainly does not believe that what Romulus did was just. But he is willing, in this particular and limited case, to excuse what Romulus did, not because it was just but because excusing an action means to recognize that an action is wrong but was committed under extraordinary circumstances that attenuate its wrongness. Justification of immoral actions in general implies that no moral values exist; excusing an individual immoral action maintains a belief in a system of moral values, but finds an exception to such general rules in the practical conduct of an individual in a single case.

best not to name: most likely a reference to Ferdinand I of Aragon and V of Castile and Leon.

64 *few had a good end*: Machiavelli devotes the longest chapter of the *Discourses on Livy* (3. 6) to conspiracies.

64 *to find him*: Sante Bentivoglio.

65 *the lives and deaths of some Roman emperors*: Machiavelli concentrates upon the period between AD 161 and 238. His source is Herodian's Greek history, translated into Latin by Angelo Poliziano and published in 1493.

68 *Under this pretext*: Machiavelli uses the word 'colour' (translated as 'pretext'), associating colouring over the truth with deception.

69 *a large part of the populace of Rome and all that of Alexandria*: obviously an exaggeration, but Herodian does report the murders of numerous Romans and a massacre in Alexandria.

70 *except the Turk and the Sultan*: the Turk is Selim I, Ottoman ruler 1512–20. He defeated the Sultan (Tuman Bey), the last Mameluk ruler of Egypt, in 1517.

73 *like an appendage*: see Chapters I and III for a definition of this kind of state.

when Italy enjoyed a balance of power: historians of political thought often credit Francesco Guicciardini's *History of Italy* (1561–4) with the concept of the balance of power. This view of the interrelationships between sovereign states focuses upon the period from the Peace of Lodi (1454) to the French invasion of Italy by King Charles VIII of France in 1494. During this relatively happy and stable period, the Italian powers (Florence, Milan, Venice, the Papal States, Naples, and the other duchies and small city-states of the peninsula) based their foreign policies on the concept of the balance of power, creating alliances when any one power seemed to be gaining hegemony. From Machiavelli's remark, it is clear that the notion was one shared by other thinkers before it was popularized by Guicciardini's influential history.

the Guelf and Ghibelline sects: here Machiavelli uses the word for sect (*sette*), not other terms he employs for factions (*divisioni, parte*). In the Middle Ages the Guelfs favoured the papacy while Ghibellines supported the emperor. By Machiavelli's day, however, these terms meant very little, and had become a convenient means of identifying opposing factions.

at Vailà: 14 May 1509, also known as the battle of Agnadello. Troops from the League of Cambrai defeated the Venetian land forces at this important battle.

the entire territory: Venice lost territory on the mainland (including the important cities of Brescia, Verona, Vicenza, and Padua), but not any important possessions in her overseas empire, the source of her commercial wealth.

75 *to hold that state*: in 1482.

to recapture that state: driven out of Urbino by Borgia in June 1502, he returned in October 1502, only to be driven out again in January 1503, after Borgia's execution of the conspirators against him at Senigallia. He finally returned to Urbino in August 1503, when Pope Alexander VI died.

75   *after returning to power in Bologna*: driven out of Bologna by Pope Julius II in 1506, the Bentivoglio returned to the city in 1511.

The castle of Milan that Francesco Sforza built there: Sforza began to construct the Castello Sforzesco immediately after his rise to power in 1450.

in order to regain her state: Machiavelli discusses Caterina Sforza Riario again in the *Discourses on Livy* (3. 6) and the *Florentine Histories* (8. 34). During a diplomatic mission to Forlì in 1499 Machiavelli met this extraordinary woman.

76   *he attacked Granada*: the Moorish kingdom in the south of Spain. Ferdinand began his attacks in 1481, and they terminated in the liberation of all of Spain from the Moors in 1492.

has since brought him honour: while Ferdinand liberated Granada with traditional forces, on 5 October 1495, he instituted a national army, and it was such an army of his own subjects that would win fame for Spanish arms in Europe during the sixteenth century.

always employing religion for his own purposes: in fact Ferdinand turned his wars against the Moors into a religious crusade against the infidel.

chasing the Marranos out of his kingdom and seizing their property: both Jews and Moors (or *moriscos*) who were forcibly converted to Christianity were called '*Marranos*', a term that might best be translated as 'swine', since it makes a derogatory reference to the pigs that neither Jews nor Muslims would eat. The Spanish Inquisition began persecution of the *Marranos* in 1483 even before the conquest of Granada in 1492. Machiavelli combines this conquest and the 1492 expulsion of the Jews from Spain with the expulsion of the *Marranos*, which took place a few years later in 1501–2. In addition to being driven into exile, the property of the exiles was confiscated and added to that of the Crown. A number of the Spanish Jews migrated to Italy, and Machiavelli no doubt met some of them.

attacked Africa: Ferdinand occupied various cities in North Africa for a time—Oran in 1509, Bugia in 1510, Tripoli in 1511. This was done to prevent a staging of a counter-attack against southern Spain, but also for religious reasons.

the invasion of Italy: Ferdinand divided the Kingdom of Naples with King Louis XII of France in 1503, taking the entire kingdom in 1505.

Lately, he attacked France: the word 'lately' indicates that Machiavelli refers here to Spain's participation in the Holy League in 1512, an alliance Pope Julius II organized against the French to defend, at least in theory, the unity of the Church. This word also convinces many scholars that this passage must have been written before 1513.

77 *Messer Bernabò Visconti of Milan*: this ruler was famous for the severity and cruelty of his punishments.

vitoris eritis: Livy, 35. 49. Machiavelli's Latin text differs slightly from the current critical editions.

78 *against the Duke of Milan*: in 1499.

in their downfall: their defeat at the battle of Vailà or Agnadello in 1509 by the French and the troops in the League of Cambrai.

to attack Lombardy: Machiavelli opposed the temporizing policies of his superior, Piero Soderini. In 1511–12, during the formation of the Holy League by Pope Julius II, Florence did not support her traditional ally France, and even tolerated a council being held in nearby Pisa set up to depose the Pope. But she also did not really support the Pope and the Spanish. The result was the sack of Prato in 1512 by a Spanish army, the downfall of Soderini's republican government, Machiavelli's dismissal from political office as Soderini's close confidant and assistant, and the return of the Medici to rule Florence in 1512.

a lover of the virtues: here the word *virtù* is given a literary and artistic twist.

in a particular skill: Machiavelli again employs the word *arte* here (see n. to p. 50).

79 *enrich his city or state*: here the term *stato* refers to the territory surrounding and including the city-state, and takes on a geographical as well as a political connotation.

into guilds: the technical term for guild is *arte*. In the traditional medieval city state, guild membership was required for political participation in the republican government, and it was usually limited to the well-to-do, not the rank-and-file labourers (thus, a guild was very unlike a modern labour union).

or neighbourhoods: Machiavelli writes *tribù* (literally 'tribes'), but he means neighbourhoods or *quartieri* into which cities like Florence are still divided today. Such districts usually depended upon the major church in that area.

Of the prince's private secretaries: Chapter XXII discusses functionaries who serve the prince as administrative officers, something between a modern minister and a Renaissance secretary such as Machiavelli. Chapter XXIII focuses upon a different kind of adviser, generally one without a precise administration position, such as a trusted courtier or businessman.

three kinds of intelligence: Machiavelli actually writes 'three kinds of brains'. He could have found this classification in a number of places, including: Hesiod, *Works and Days* (293–7); Livy (22. 20); and Cicero's speech *Pro Cluentio* (31). The idea was widespread enough during Machiavelli's day to be classified as a commonplace.

80 *the courts are full*: the problem of distinguishing honest advisers from flatterers was a much-discussed topic in the *de regimine principum* literature that preceded Machiavelli's *The Prince*. In addition, Castiglione's *Book of the Courtier* (4. 6) contains an influential treatment of this question.

83 *the King of Naples, the Duke of Milan*: Frederick I of Aragon and Ludovico Sforza of Milan.

enough strength: here Machiavelli employs the word *nervo* (nerve) for strength.

by Titus Quinctius: Philip V of Macedon.

nevertheless remained: after the battle of Cynoscephalae (197 BC), Philip V of Macedon lost his Greek possessions and was forced to pay heavy fines and give members of his family as hostages to the victors, but he retained Macedon.

84 *the other half, or almost that, to us*: Machiavelli's declaration seems based on his dilemma-like literary style (his habitual either/or construction), rather than any empirical evidence. Certainly he provides no historical evidence for asserting that men control one-half of their destiny.

no well-ordered virtue: here Machiavelli writes *ordinata virtù*, combining two of his favourite political terms to indicate that the ability of the prince needs to be channelled into institutions that may stand up to Fortune's irrational force.

85 *the variation of the good*: that is to say, the sudden shifts from good fortune to bad.

86 *was still alive*: in 1506. Julius was forced to retake the city in 1512. Machiavelli witnessed his first triumphant procession through Bologna in 1506.

brevity of his life: here and elsewhere, when Machiavelli mentions the brevity of the lives of the popes, he means to underline the brevity of their tenure as popes, not their complete life-span.

when the two are in harmony: Fortune and their means of procedure.

87 *in a single individual*: here Machiavelli probably means Cesare Borgia.

88 *to the plundering of Lombardy*: the French plundered Tortona in 1499 and Brescia in 1512.

the extortions: the *taglie* were extortions paid to besieging troops by the inhabitants of cities to avoid being sacked and pillaged after a successful siege.

of which it is now prince: on 21 February 1513 Giovanni de' Medici was elected to the papacy, taking the name Leo X.

. . . in armis spes est: Livy, 9. 1.

for your greatness: Machiavelli's images are taken from the Book of

Exodus, where prodigious events during the flight of the Hebrews from Egypt to the Promised Land are described.

89 *in the heads*: that is, the mass of Italians have ability but Italy's leaders lack it.

and Mestre: in order, the Italian defeats by foreign troops are: Fornovo on the Taro River, a French victory by the troops of King Charles VIII against an Italian alliance (6 July 1495); the conquest of Alessandria (a city in Piedmont), by the French and the surrender of Galeazzo da Sanseverino (28 August 1499); the sacking of Capua by the French (24 July 1501); the suppression of a revolt in Genoa against the French (28 April 1507); the battle of Vailà or Agnadello, where the French defeated the Venetians (14 May 1509); the capture of Bologna by the French (20 May 1511); and finally the destruction of Mestre and the defeat of Venetian forces by the Spanish (7 October 1513).

with Italian virtue: Machiavelli writes *italica virtù*.

90 *the battle of Ravenna*: on 11 April 1512.

bucklers: small round shields with a spike in the centre.

in Italian hearts: the poem comes from the *Canzoniere* of Francesco Petrarca (no. 128, ll. 93–6). The poem, known to all Italian schoolchildren as 'Italia mia', had been written to denounce the depredations of a German mercenary soldier near Parma in 1344–55, and because of its theme and its call for Italian unity, it made for a perfect and familiar literary conclusion to Machiavelli's treatise.

GLOSSARY OF PROPER NAMES

Achilles: legendary warrior hero of Homer's *Iliad* educated by Chiron the centaur.

Agathocles: (361–289 BC), ruler of Syracuse after 317 BC who eventually controlled most of Sicily and waged war successfully against the Carthaginians, carrying the battle into Africa after being besieged inside the city of Syracuse.

Alberigo of Conio: (1348–1409), Alberigo da Barbiano, mercenary leader and Count of Conio in the Romagna, who fought at various times for the papacy, Bernarbò Visconti, Gian Galeazzo Visconti, and the Kingdom of Naples. Concerned about the devastation in Italy caused by foreign mercenaries, he formed a military company called the Company of Saint George that admitted only Italians. Because of his practices, most mercenary soldiers in Italy by the end of the fourteenth century were Italian *condottieri*.

Albinus: Decimus Clodius Albinus was governor of Britain when Emperor Commodus died in AD 192; Severus defeated him near Lyons in 197 and brought him back to Rome, where he was beheaded.

Alexander, Emperor: (AD 208–35), M. Aurelius Alexander Severus, Roman emperor (222–35), adopted by his cousin the Emperor Heliogabalus and proclaimed emperor after Heliogabalus' assassination. While considered a just ruler, he was murdered by mutinous troops in Gaul where he had gone to fight German invasions.

Alexander the Great: (356–323 BC), Alexander III, King of Macedon, antiquity's greatest military leader, and son of Philip II of Macedon. After succeeding his father in 336 BC, Alexander crossed the Hellespont in 334, defeated Darius III of Persia, and reached India in 327.

Alexander VI, Pope: Rodrigo Borgia (1431–1503, elected pope in 1492), a Spaniard from Aragon, Borgia earned a degree in canon law at the University of Bologna and was made a cardinal in 1456 by his uncle, Cardinal Alfonso de Borja, who was elected Pope Calixtus III in 1455. His son Cesare (Duke Valentino) and his daughter Lucrezia (1480–1519) were important personalities in Renaissance Italy, and Borgia's papacy was noted for its corruption, ambition, and able administration. The Pope desired to use the papacy to assist his son Cesare in establishing a hereditary power-base in Italy for the Borgia family, but their well-laid plans (admired by Machiavelli) came to naught when the Pope died suddenly while his son was ill.

Alfonso V of Aragon, also Alfonso I of Naples: (1395–1458), King of Aragon in 1416 and ruler of Sicily after 1420. Queen Giovanna II of Naples adopted him as her heir, but later chose Louis III of Aragon as her successor. After the death of Louis, Alfonso defeated Louis's brother René in 1443 and subsequently made his court in Naples a celebrated centre of culture during his reign.

Amboise, Georges D', Cardinal of Rouen: (1460–1510), one of the most able of French political figures, who became a bishop at the age of 14 and archbishop of Rouen in 1493, receiving the cardinal's hat in 1498 as a result of a deal between King Louis XII of France and Pope Alexander VI. Amboise was the chief minister for Louis XII and was especially concerned with matters involving Italy. One of the important candidates for the papacy in the elections of 1503 after Alexander VI's death, Amboise played a role in French diplomacy until the end of his life.

Antiochus III 'The Great': King of Syria and ruler of what was known as the Seleucid Empire (223–187 BC). Invited by the Aetolians (a confederation of cities and states in Greece), Antiochus invaded Greece in 196, but was defeated there by the Romans at the battles of Thermopylae in 191 and Magnesia in 190. The subsequent Peace of Apamea in 188 ended his adventures in Greece and confined his domain to Asia Minor, making Rome the dominant power in the Greek peninsula.

Ascanio, Cardinal: Ascanio Sforza (1455–1505), son of Francesco Sforza, brother of Ludovico 'Il Moro', and a powerful cleric, who became cardinal in 1484 and used his influence in the papacy to assist his father. He was a strong candidate during the papal election that elected Cardinal Rodrigo Borgia to the papacy as Alexander VI. He helped to arrange the marriage of Borgia's daughter, Lucrezia, to Giovanni Sforza, the ruler of Pesaro, a union that was annulled in 1497. But the Pope and the Cardinal eventually fell out, and when King Louis XII of France invaded Italy and took Milan from his brother Ludovico, Ascanio was captured by the French in 1500.

Bentivoglio, Annibale I: (1413–45), mercenary soldier and ruler of Bologna from 1443 until his assassination.

Bentivoglio, Annibale II: (1469–1540), son of Giovanni II Bentivoglio and a mercenary soldier who often served Florence.

Bentivoglio, Giovanni II: (1443–1508), son of Annibale I and ruler of Bologna after the death of Sante Bentivoglio in 1463. He was driven out of Bologna in 1506 by troops led by Pope Julius II and died in Milan.

Bentivoglio, Sante: (1426–63), illegitimate son of Ercole Bentivoglio, who was found working in the Florentine wool industry after Annibale I was assassinated in Bologna and brought back to Bologna to rule there in 1446, with the support of the government of Florence and the favour of the people of Bologna. He ruled the city successfully until his death.

Bergamo, Bartolomeo da: (1400–75), Bartolomeo Colleoni, mercenary soldier from Bergamo, who served Naples, Florence, Venice, and Milan at various times in his illustrious career. From 1454 until his death he was the commander of Venetian armies and was considered one of the greatest Italian *condottieri* of the period. Andrea del Verrocchio's famous equestrian statue of Colleoni stands today in the Campo Santi Giovanni e Paolo in Venice, and is one of the greatest equestrian statues produced during the Italian Renaissance.

Borgia, Cesare: (1475–1507), son of Cardinal Rodrigo Borgia (later Pope Alexander VI) and Vannozza Catanei. Like his father, Cesare studied canon law in Italy at Perugia and Pisa, became archbishop of Valencia when his father was elected Pope, and was made a cardinal by his father in 1493. Pedro Luiz, the son that the Pope had destined for a secular career, died in 1488, and the Pope's other son Juan was murdered in 1497. Cesare therefore renounced his position as cardinal and received from King Louis XII of France the title of Duke of Valentinois (hence, the name Duke Valentino, by which he was known to Machiavelli and the Italians). Returning to Italy in 1499, Cesare began to attack a number of rulers in the Papal States as the captain-general of the papal army, capturing Fano, Pesaro, Rimini, Cesena, Faenza, Imola, and Forlì. Named Duke of the Romagna by Alexander, Cesare planned to attack Camerino and Urbino. In 1502 he thwarted a plot by his mercenary allies and executed the ringleaders after tricking them into a meeting at Senigallia. When his father fell ill in 1503, Cesare tried to hold on to power by supporting the election of Julius II. When this move failed he fled to Naples, where he was arrested by the Spanish viceroy and returned to Spain and imprisoned; but after escaping he served the

King of Navarre as a soldier and died in an obscure skirmish in 1507 at the age of 32. Machiavelli observed Borgia several times in 1502 and 1503, as a diplomatic representative of the Republic of Florence, both before and after his fall from grace. His praise of the man's political and military successes later left Machiavelli open to charges of immorality, since the most popular historical work of the European Renaissance, Francesco Guicciardini's *History of Italy* (1569), popularized the scandalous rumours spread by Spanish-hating Italians that the Borgia family—Pope Alexander, his son Cesare, and his daughter Lucrezia—engaged in incestuous sexual relationships. For his part, Machiavelli obviously heard the rumours during the times he observed Borgia in Italy and recognized them for the calumnies they actually were, but his praise of Borgia continued to remain as one of the primary causes for the association of Machiavelli's *The Prince* with immorality, particularly in the non-Catholic Protestant nations of the north.

Borgia, Rodrigo: *see* Alexander VI, Pope.

Braccio da Montone: (1368–1424), Andrea Fortebraccio, mercenary soldier from Perugia, who seized power in that city in 1416 and ruled it until his death from wounds at the battle of Aquila.

Caesar, Julius: (100–44 BC), Roman military leader who conquered Gaul and made himself dictator of Rome before his assassination by Brutus and a number of republican leaders.

Canneschi family, the: members of a powerful Bolognese family that opposed Bentivoglio rule in Bologna and were a factor in the successful assassination of Annibale I Bentivoglio in 1445.

Caracalla, Marcus Aurelius Antoninus, Emperor: (AD 188–217), son of Emperor Septimius Severus. After Severus's death in 211, Caracalla murdered his brother Geta to obtain imperial power. One of his most important acts was to extend Roman citizenship to all free citizens of the empire. He was assassinated by Macrinus, prefect of his praetorian guard, who succeeded him.

Carmagnola: (*c.*1385–1432), Francesco Bussone, Count of Carmagnola, a celebrated mercenary leader from Piedmont who served Filippo, Duke of Milan, for many years but later fled to Venice to serve the Duke's major adversary, where he became the Venetian commander. Because of his continued ties to Milan, Venetians suspected him of treachery and had him beheaded.

Charles VII, King of France: (1403–61), French ruler, during whose reign the Hundred Years War ended in 1453, with the English holding only the port city of Calais. Machiavelli believed his policies on military and financial matters gave France a strong, centralized military force under the King's direct control.

Charles VIII, King of France: (1470–98), son of Louis XI and the last of the Valois rulers of France. He invaded Italy in September 1494 because he asserted the House of Anjou's claim to the Kingdom of Naples. In this invasion he was supported by Ludovico Sforza, 'Il Moro', who thought the French would enable him to seize some Venetian territory. After Charles took Naples in 1495 an Italian League (composed of Venice, Milan, Spain, Pope Alexander VI, and the German emperor) formed to oppose his designs. The allied forces failed to destroy the outnumbered French army on the Taro River at the battle of Fornovo in 1495, allowing Charles to return to France. Subsequently, in 1496, Naples was lost to the French. Charles died before he could complete the second Italian invasion he was planning at the time of his death. He was succeeded by his cousin Louis, Duke of Orléans, who became King Louis XII.

Chiron the centaur: in Greek mythology centaurs were represented with the head and torso of a man and the body of a horse. While they were often considered to be brutal and lecherous, some, like Chiron, were wise. Chiron became the adviser and teacher of Achilles, the legendary Homeric warrior, during his childhood.

Clement VII, Pope, Giulio de' Medici: (1478–1534), illegitimate son of Giuliano de' Medici (the brother of Lorenzo de' Medici, 'The Magnificent'), who was killed in the Pazzi Plot in 1478. When Giulio's cousin Giovanni de' Medici was elected to the papacy as Leo X in 1513, Giulio was made a cardinal. When Lorenzo de' Medici, Duke of Urbino (and the man to whom *The Prince* was dedicated), died in 1519, the Cardinal became the de facto ruler of Florence until he was elected pope in 1523, taking the name Clement VII. As Cardinal, Giulio commissioned Machiavelli to write the *Florentine Histories*, a work Machiavelli brought to Clement VII in Rome in 1525. Clement's attempts to oppose the Emperor Charles V in Italy met with disaster: the League of Cognac the Pope formed with Florence, Venice, and the Duke of Milan resulted in the fall of Medici power in Florence in 1527 and the Sack of Rome in that year.

Colonna family, the: a powerful Roman family dating from the thirteenth century that frequently opposed the policies of a strong papacy, and were particularly hostile to Pope Alexander VI, who

confiscated their properties and excommunicated them, to no
avail.

Colonna, Giovanni, Cardinal: (d. 1508), created a cardinal in 1480
by Pope Sixtus IV, Cardinal Colonna joined forces with Cardinal
Giuliano della Rovere (later Pope Julius II) and others in urging
King Charles VIII of France to depose Pope Alexander VI. Besides
such international intrigue, the Cardinal also found time to oppose
the Orsini family, the traditional enemies of the Colonna family.

Commodus, Lucius Aelius Aurelius, Emperor: (AD 161–92),
following his popular father Marcus Aurelius as supreme ruler of
Rome in 180, Commodus soon became a cruel and oppressive ruler.
He enjoyed taking part in gladiatorial contests. He was murdered by
a number of people in his court who discovered that he had planned
to have them assassinated.

Cyrus the Great: founder of the Persian Empire, he conquered the
Medes in around 549 BC.

Darius III, King of Persia: (380–330 BC), the last king of Persia,
Darius was defeated by Alexander the Great at the battles of Issus
(333 BC) and Gangamela or Arbela (331). He was assassinated by a
relative when he fled to the eastern part of his empire.

David: (ninth century BC), as a young shepherd boy David slew the
Philistine giant Goliath (an act that became an important iconic
symbol for Florentine republicanism in the art of Donatello and
Michelangelo) and succeeded King Saul to the throne of Israel.

Dido: the unhappy Queen of Carthage in Virgil's *Aeneid*, who falls in
love with the Trojan prince Aeneas and commits suicide when he
abandons her to follow his mission of founding Rome.

Emperor of Constantinople, the: John VI Cantacuzene (c.1292–
1383), who ruled the Byzantine Empire from 1341 to 1355 after
usurping the throne from John V Palaeologus, who eventually
regained his throne in 1354. He was responsible for bringing the
Ottoman Turks into the Byzantine civil wars.

Epaminondas: (c.418–362 BC), Theban general and politician who
played a large role in the defeat of the Spartans at the battle of
Leuctra (371); he died in the battle of Mantinea. As a result of his
policies, Thebes gained her independence as a Greek city-state.

Este, Alfonso I D', Duke of Ferrara: (1476–1534), son of Ercole I,
Alfonso became Duke of Ferrara in 1505. After the death of his wife
Anna Sforza, in 1502 he married Lucrezia Borgia, daughter of Pope
Alexander VI. He refused to join the Venetians and the Pope in the

Holy League against the French. He was one of the best soldiers of his era, during which time Ferrara produced some of the best cannon of the period. In spite of the vigorous efforts of other Italian powers, and especially a succession of popes, to dislodge him from Ferrara, Alfonso maintained power in that city by his talents as a diplomat, soldier, and statesman.

Este, Ercole I D', Duke of Ferrara: (1431–1505), after becoming ruler of Ferrara in 1471, Ercole produced one of Europe's most brilliant courts, where poets such as Boiardo and Ariosto were protected and supported. Ercole also made clever marriages, uniting his daughter Isabella d'Este to the Marquis of Mantua, Gian Francesco Gonzaga, and his other daughter Beatrice d'Este to Ludovico Sforza, 'Il Moro'. These marriages were important to Ercole's political relationships with other Italian powers.

Fabius Maximus: (Quintus Fabius Maximus), Roman consul made dictator in 217 BC. His delaying tactics against Hannibal while the Carthaginian army ravaged Italy were opposed by Scipio, who preferred waging a more aggressive campaign.

Ferdinand II of Aragon and V of Castile and Leon: (1452–1516), married to his cousin Isabella of Castile, Ferdinand became King of Aragon in 1479 and drove the Moors out of Spain by 1492. He agreed to divide the Kingdom of Naples (then ruled by his cousin, King Frederick I of Aragon) with King Louis XII of France in the Treaty of Granada (11 November 1500), but the two monarchs later disagreed over the division of the spoils. After a number of military defeats, the French recognized Ferdinand as King of Naples in the Treaty of Blois (12 October 1505).

Ferrara, Duke of: *see* Este, Alfonso I D' and Este, Ercole I D'.

Fogliani, Giovanni: the ruler of the city of Fermo and the uncle of Oliverotto of Fermo, Fogliani was murdered by his nephew in 1502, along with his son and several others of his supporters.

Forlì, Countess of: Caterina Sforza Riario (1463–1509), daughter of Galeazzo Maria Sforza, Duke of Milan, and niece of Ludovico Sforza, 'Il Moro'. Caterina married Girolamo Riario, ruler of Forlì and Imola, in 1477 and defended Forlì from its famous fortress until her uncle sent assistance. Later in 1499–1500 Cesare Borgia captured both Forlì and Imola from her, and after being imprisoned in Rome, she died in a convent.

Fortebraccio, Andrea: *see* Braccio (da Montone).

Frederick I of Aragon, King of Naples: (1452–1504), becoming ruler of the kingdom in 1496, Frederick was the target of the Treaty of Granada (1500) by which his cousin King Ferdinand II of Spain and King Louis XII of France agreed to conquer his kingdom and divide it between them. After he lost his kingdom as a result of their combined attacks from north (France) and south (Spain), he went into exile in France, where he died in 1504. The French recognized Ferdinand II of Spain as King of Naples in the Treaty of Blois in 1505.

Giovanna II, Queen of Naples: (1371–1435), ruler of Naples from 1414 until her death, who hired mercenaries to defend her kingdom. She named first King Alfonso V of Aragon and then Louis III of Aragon as her successor, and after the death of Louis, she chose his brother René. Her erratic actions plunged the kingdom into a political crisis that was exploited by other European powers.

Girolamo, Count: husband of the Countess of Forlì, Girolamo Riario, ruler of Forlì and Imola, murdered in 1488 because of his oppressive rule. In 1477 he married Caterina Sforza.

Goliath: the Philistine giant slain by David in the Old Testament narrative recounted in 1 Samuel.

Gonzaga, Gian Francesco, Marquis of Mantua: (1466–1519), mercenary leader who succeeded his father Federico in 1484 as ruler of Mantua. He married Isabella d'Este in 1490. He commanded various armies, including the Venetian forces.

Gracchi, the: two Roman brothers—Tiberius Sempronius Gracchus (d. 133 BC) and Gaius Sepronius Gracchus (d. 121 BC). Both men were tribunes of the plebs and popular reformers. They both died in upheavals instigated in Republican Rome by their aristocratic opponents, who opposed their plans for agrarian reform.

Guido Baldo, Duke of Urbino: (1472–1508), the son of celebrated *condottiere* and ruler of Urbino, Duke Federico II of Montefeltro (1422–82), and Battista Sforza, Guidobaldo da Montefeltro succeeded Federico as Duke of Urbino upon his father's death. He was driven out of Urbino by Cesare Borgia in 1502 but returned during the same year. The brilliance of his court inspired an elegiac portrait of it in *The Book of the Courtier* by Baldesar Castiglione (1528). The last of the Montefeltro line of dukes in Urbino, he was succeeded by Francesco Maria Della Rovere (1490–1538), whose family ruled Urbino until 1631.

Hamilcar the Carthaginian: father of Hannibal, Hamilcar Barca was commander of the Carthaginian forces in Sicily during the First Punic War.

Hannibal: (249–183 BC), commander of the Carthaginian army during the Second Punic War. After crossing the Alps and attacking Roman territory, where he inflicted massive losses on Roman armies, he was finally defeated by Scipio at the battle of Zama in 202 BC, bringing the war to a close. He eventually committed suicide to avoid falling into Roman hands, after fleeing from Carthage to a number of cities in Asia Minor.

Hawkwood, Sir John: (1320–94), English mercenary soldier, known to Italians as Giovanni Acuto. After service in France, where he was knighted by Edward III of England, Hawkwood went to Italy in 1360 with a small band of his soldiers and became one of Italy's most famous *condottieri*. He served the Republic of Florence from 1380 until his death, and is remembered in the Florentine Cathedral with a fresco painted by Paolo Uccello in 1436.

Heliogabalus, Emperor: (*c.* AD 205–22), ruler of Rome between 218 and 222, until his assassination by his praetorian guard.

Hiero of Syracuse: (*c.*308–216 BC), elected ruler of the Greek city state of Syracuse in Sicily by its citizens in 270. During the First Punic War he first supported the Carthaginians, but then, after 263, allied himself with Rome. This policy guaranteed his control of Syracuse until his death.

Julian, Emperor: (d. AD 193), Marcus Didius Salvius Julianus, the son of a Roman general who became emperor after the assassination of Pertinax by the praetorian guards, who offered the imperial crown to the highest bidder. He ruled for less than a year and was executed and replaced by Septimius Severus.

Julius II, Pope (Giuliano della Rovere): (1443–1513), nephew of Pope Sixtus IV, Giuliano della Rovere became first Cardinal of St Peter's in Chains in Rome, then was elevated to the papacy as Julius II in 1503. One of the greatest of Renaissance popes, Julius II is famous for his patronage of Michelangelo, Raphael, and Bramante, and for the initial plans to rebuild old St Peter's Basilica. His policies were driven by an impetuous character, but he succeeded in restoring papal control to a number of cities in central Italy that had been taken over by local lords (such as the Bentivoglio family in Bologna or the Baglioni family in Perugia). The Holy League, an anti-French alliance formed by his diplomacy, resulted in a famous military defeat at Ravenna (1512), where Swiss soldiers nevertheless forced a French withdrawal, saving the Pope from disaster.

Leo X, Pope (Giovanni de' Medici): (1475–1521), the son of Lorenzo de' Medici, 'The Magnificent', Giovanni de' Medici was appointed to the rank of cardinal by Pope Innocent VIII in 1492. Elected Pope in 1513 as Leo X, it was his misfortune to become embroiled in the controversies with Martin Luther over indulgences. Leo excommunicated Luther in 1521 just before his death, marking the beginning of the Protestant Reformation. Leo was a generous patron of humanists and artists. He appointed a number of his relatives to high church offices and had his nephew Lorenzo de' Medici (the man to whom Machiavelli wrote his second and final dedication of *The Prince*) named Duke of Urbino.

Louis XI, King of France: (1423–83), Louis became king in 1461 and added a number of territories to the French Crown. Machiavelli disliked his military policy, which embraced the hiring of Swiss mercenary infantrymen after 1474.

Louis XII, King of France: (1462–1515), first Duke of Orléans, then king in 1498, following the death of Charles VIII. During his reign he was heavily involved in Italian affairs, making claims against both Milan and Naples on the basis of hereditary connections to various noble families there. He made a deal with Pope Alexander VI to annul his marriage to Jeanne, daughter of Louis XI, so that he could marry the widow of Charles VIII, Anne of Brittany, thereby annexing that region to his kingdom. After allying himself with Venice, he invaded Lombardy, asserting a claim to the duchy of Milan, and drove Ludovico Sforza out of the city for a time, although Sforza managed to return in 1500. In the Treaty of Granada of 1500 he agreed to divide the Kingdom of Naples with the Spanish, and that region was invaded by him in 1501. Subsequently, however, the Spanish and the French quarrelled and Louis lost Naples. Louis then joined with the Pope, Spain, and the Empire to attack the Venetians in the League of Cambrai. Venice was defeated in 1509 at the battle of Agnadello or Vailà. Pope Julius II then formed the Holy League against his forces in Italy, and even though his army defeated their opponents at the battle of Ravenna in 1512, his great commander Gaston de Foix was killed. Later, in 1513, Louis concluded an alliance with Venice against the Milanese, but this time his forces were defeated at the battle of Novara by Swiss troops.

Luca, Father: Luca Rainaldi, an ambassador for Emperor Maximilian.

Ludovico Il Moro: *see* Sforza, Ludovico.

Macrinus, Emperor: (*c.* AD 164–218), born in North Africa, Macrinus first served Septimius Severus and then became a prefect of the praetorian guard under Caracalla, after whose death in 217 he was proclaimed emperor, a post he held for only one short year.

Mantua, Marquis of: *see* Gian Francesco Gonzaga.

Marcus Aurelius, Emperor: (AD 121–80), Roman ruler from 161 until his death. A stoic philosopher and author of a famous book of *Meditations* written in Greek, he spent much of his reign governing wisely and well, but also engaged in border wars along the distant frontiers of the now-threatened empire.

Maximilian I, Emperor: (1459–1519), son of Emperor Frederick III, Maximilian was elected King of the Romans (German king) in 1485, and in 1508 assumed the title of Holy Roman Emperor with the tacit consent of Pope Julius II. Machiavelli visited his court on a diplomatic mission in 1508 and was little impressed by his character, judging him too indecisive to amount to much. In 1494 Maximilian married Bianca Maria Sforza, daughter of Galeazzo Sforza, the late Duke of Milan. As sole ruler of Germany and the head of the Habsburg family, his ambitions were fulfilled by his grandson, who succeeded him as Emperor Charles V.

Maximinus, Emperor: (d. AD 238), ruler of Rome for a brief time (235–8), Gaius Julius Verus Maximinus came to power from humble origins as a Thracian centurion. He was murdered by his own troops.

Medici, Lorenzo de', the Magnificent: although Machiavelli dedicates *The Prince* to this individual, he is not Lorenzo de' Medici 'the Magnificent' (1449–92), the grandson of Cosimo de' Medici and one of the most brilliant political leaders of the Quattrocento, but a rather insignificant Medici princeling of the same name, called by Machiavelli in his dedication 'The Magnificent' to compliment him. Machiavelli was forced to change his first dedication to Giuliano de' Medici, Duke of Nemours (1479–1516), after the latter's sudden death. Lorenzo died three years after becoming Duke of Urbino. The fact that both of the Medici princelings to whom Machiavelli dedicated his treatise died early may well explain why Machiavelli did not publish *The Prince* during his lifetime. Lorenzo, Duke of Urbino (1492–1519), was the son of Piero de' Medici

(1471–1503, ruler of Florence between 1492 and 1494), and the grandson of the more famous Lorenzo the Magnificent. After Duke Francesco Maria della Rovere was driven out of Urbino in 1516, Pope Leo X named Lorenzo the new duke. He was the father of Alessandro de' Medici (1510–37), assassinated after becoming the first Medici duke of Florence, and of Catherine de' Medici (1519–89), the wife of Henry II of France. Michelangelo constructed tombs for both the Duke of Nemours and the Duke of Urbino under the New Sacristy of the Church of San Lorenzo in Florence.

Moses: lawgiver and Hebrew leader, who led the Israelites out of captivity in Egypt to within sight of the Promised Land.

Nabis: (*c*.240–192 BC), ruler of Sparta who took power in 207 BC, but was defeated in several battles by Romans and by Philopoemen, head of the Achaean League. He was subsequently assassinated.

Oliverotto of Fermo: (1475–1502), Oliviero or Oliverotto Euffreducci, a mercenary soldier born in Fermo in the Marches, who was raised by his uncle, Giovanni Fogliani. He fought as a soldier with Paulo Vitelli and subsequently with Vitellozzo Vitelli after the Florentine government executed Paulo in 1499 for treachery. Vitellozzo Vitelli's troops served under Cesare Borgia. Oliverotto seized power in Fermo in 1501 and then joined in a conspiracy against Borgia. Cesare tricked the plotters, had them arrested at Senigallia, and at the end of 1502 Oliverotto and his co-conspirator Vitellozzo were strangled on Borgia's orders.

Orco, Remirro Del: (Ramiro de Lorqua), a Spaniard in the service of Cesare Borgia, appointed governor of the Romagna in 1501 by him. In 1502 Borgia ordered him murdered and his dismembered body publicly displayed in Cesena, in the hope of winning favour from the fickle population of the Romagna.

Orsini family, the: a noble Roman family with origins in the thirteenth century. The Orsini were the traditional enemies of the Colonna family in Rome, and like them they frequently opposed the growing power of the papacy, unless that office was held by a person friendly to their clan. A number of Orsini served as mercenary leaders during Machiavelli's lifetime.

Orsini, Paulo: (1460–1503), a mercenary soldier who fought at various times for Florence, Venice, and Cesare Borgia. Borgia tricked Paulo and others into meeting him at Senigallia in December of 1502, where he had them all arrested and eventually murdered.

Paulo was one of the last conspirators strangled, along with his cousin, Francesco Orsini, Duke of Gravina, in January 1503.

Pertinax, Emperor: (AD 129–93), Publius Helvius Pertinax, Roman emperor from Liguria who was made leader of the empire upon the assassination of Commodus by the praetorian guard in January 193, but whose attempts to discipline the soldiers led to his assassination only two months later.

Pescennius Niger: upon the assassination of Commodus in AD 192, Pescennius Niger was proclaimed emperor in the east by the Roman soldiers stationed there, but in 194 Septimius Severus defeated him in battle at Issus in Asia Minor and had him executed in that year.

Petrarch: (1304–74), Francesco Petrarca, Italy's greatest lyric poet and humanist scholar, whose ideas about which books from the classical tradition ought to be read were to form the basis for education in Europe for many centuries. Machiavelli's concluding chapter of *The Prince* cites one of Petrarch's most famous poems.

Petrucci, Pandolfo: (1450–1512), ruler of Siena, with whom Machiavelli negotiated on several occasions as a representative of the Florentine Republic. Petrucci seized power in 1487, and was a conspirator against Cesare Borgia with others who, less fortunate, were murdered by Borgia when they fell into his hands at Senigallia.

Philip of Macedon: (382–336 BC), Phillip II, King of Macedon and father of Alexander the Great. He was assassinated after conquering most of Greece, as he prepared to attack the Persians, an expansionist policy his son Alexander followed and perfected.

Philip of Macedon: (238–179 BC), Philip V, King of Macedon after 221 BC, who fought several wars against the Romans. He was decisively defeated in 197 at the battle of Cynoscephalae in Thessaly by Titus Quinctius Flaminius.

Philopoemen: (253–184 BC), Greek general and head of the Achaean League who defeated Nabis, King of Sparta, a number of times.

Pitigliano, Count of: (1442–1510), Niccolò Orsini, Count of Pitigliano, mercenary leader who served the papacy, Florence, and eventually Venice, and the cousin of Paulo Orsini who was executed by Borgia in 1503. Niccolò Orsini commanded Venetian troops at the disastrous defeat at Agnadello or Vailà in 1509.

Pyrrhus: (*c*.319–272 BC), King of Epirus and accomplished general, who waged war on Rome in Italy and on Carthage in Sicily. His costly triumphs on the battlefield have given us the phrase 'pyrrhic victory'.

Riario, Cardinal Raffaello: (1452–1521), a member of a powerful family associated with the Romagna, Raffaello was made a cardinal in 1477 and was archbishop of Pisa from 1479 to 1499. In 1478 he barely escaped with his life after saying Mass in the Florentine Cathedral during the Pazzi conspiracy against the Medici that resulted in the death of Lorenzo the Magnificent's brother Giuliano. He was later implicated in a plot against the Medici Pope Leo X, but was pardoned after paying a large fine in 1517.

Romulus: according to legend and Livy's history of Rome, Romulus and Remus—two brothers abandoned to the care of a she-wolf—founded the city of Rome; Romulus subsequently murdered his brother and became Rome's first king.

Rouen, Cardinal of: *see* Amboise, Georges D'.

San Giorgio, Cardinal of: *see* Riario, Cardinal Raffaello.

Saint Peter's in Chains, Cardinal of: *see* Julius II, Pope.

San Severino, Roberto da: (1418–87), a mercenary soldier who served a number of masters in Italy, including Francesco Sforza, Ludovico Sforza, and Venice.

Saul: the first king of Israel, according to the Old Testament.

Savonarola, Brother Girolamo: (1452–98), Dominican preacher and religious reformer from Ferrara, who became Prior of San Marco in Florence. His fiery sermons, containing denunciations of contemporary corruption and prophecies of dire events in the future, attracted a huge following, and for a brief period after the expulsion of the Medici in 1494 Savonarola was also a major force behind republican politics. His *Treatise on the Organization and Government of Florence* (1498) proposed a republican government for the city and an enlarged Grand Council based on his understanding of the Venetian republic. Pope Alexander VI eventually excommunicated Savonarola and then threatened to place the city of Florence under an interdict. He was arrested, tortured, and executed in the Piazza della Signoria in 1498, but his influence among radical republicans in Florence would endure for some decades after his demise.

Scali, Giorgio: a wealthy Florentine who became head of the popular faction after the Ciompi Revolt of 1378, Scali was eventually beheaded in 1382 for leading an attack against the palace of one of the city's magistrates.

Scipio: (234–183 BC), Publius Cornelius Scipio Africanus, perhaps Rome's greatest general and the nemesis of Hannibal, commander of the Carthaginian forces. After driving the Carthaginians out of Spain by 207 BC, Scipio invaded North Africa and defeated Hannibal's forces at the epic battle of Zama in 202. For his victories, he was given the title 'Africanus'.

Severus, Emperor: (AD 146–211), Lucius Septimius Severus, Roman emperor from North Africa. After the assassination of Pertinax in 193, Severus eliminated Julian in Rome, and then defeated Pescennius Niger at Issus in 194 and Albinus in France in 196. After that time he fought campaigns against the Parthians and in Britain, where he died peacefully (one of only a few emperors to do so during the period Machiavelli analyses in *The Prince*, AD 161–238).

Sforza, Cardinal: (1455–1505), Ascanio Sforza, son of Francesco Sforza, created cardinal in 1484 and a strong supporter of his brother Ludovico Sforza, Duke of Milan. Although he supported Cardinal Rodrigo Borgia in his election to the papacy as Alexander VI, Sforza later opposed Borgia's policies.

Sforza, Francesco: (1401–66), Francesco commanded his father's mercenary soldiers after 1424 and served Duke Filippo Visconti in Milan, marrying the duke's daughter, Bianca Maria, in 1441. After Visconti's death, Sforza eventually took control of the duchy of Milan in 1450 with the assistance of Florence. The Sforzas were a powerful force in Milan and Lombardy until the foreign invasions of Italy eventually destroyed their hold on the duchy.

Sforza, Ludovico, 'Il Moro': (1451–1508), known as *Il Moro* or 'The Moor' because of his dark complexion, Ludovico was the second son of Francesco. After the assassination of his elder brother Galeazzo Maria in 1476, Ludovico eventually became regent for Galeazzo Maria's son Gian Galeazzo in 1480. Ludovico was made Duke of Milan in 1494, when Gian Galeazzo mysteriously died. Ludovico was one of the most fascinating rulers of his day: he was the patron of Leonardo da Vinci and married Beatrice d'Este (1475–97), daughter of Ercole I, Duke of Ferrara in 1491, an event that added splendour to his Milanese court. Machiavelli holds Ludovico primarily responsible for encouraging the foreign invasions of Italy through his support for the invasion of Charles VIII in 1494, in order to gain territory from Venice. However, when King Louis XII of France invaded Lombardy, claiming the duchy of Milan in 1499, Ludovico was swiftly driven out of Milan, and although he returned temporarily in 1500, he was subsequently captured in a battle near Novara in that year and spent the rest of his life as a French prisoner near Tours.

Sforza, Muzio: Muzio Attendolo Sforza (1369–1424), a mercenary soldier and father of Francesco Sforza, who fought with Alberico da Barbiano. He served under a number of masters, including Perugia, Florence, Ferrara, Milan, and Naples.

Sixtus, Pope: (1414–84), Francesco della Rovere, elected to the papacy as Sixtus IV in 1471. Like all Renaissance popes of Italian origin, Sixtus practised a policy of nepotism, giving a number of relatives appointments as cardinals, including his nephew Giuliano della Rovere, later to become the famous Pope Julius II. Because he supported the Riario family's attempts to gain power in the Romagna, he came into conflict with the Medici family of Florence and was involved in the Pazzi Conspiracy in 1478 against them. A great patron of the arts, Sixtus has given his name to the Sistine Chapel in the Vatican.

Sultan, the: by this title Machiavelli refers to the ruler of Mameluk Egypt, who was traditionally selected from among the commanders of the slave army of that state. In 1517 Selim I, the ruler of Ottoman Turkey, overthrew the Mameluks' power in Egypt, killing Tuman Bey, the last Mameluk Sultan.

Theseus: legendary Greek hero who slew the Minotaur in the labyrinth of Crete.

Titus Quinctius: (227–174 BC), Titus Quinctius Flaminius, Roman consul (198) and commander in 197 of the Roman army that defeated Philip V of Macedon at the battle of Cynoscephalae.

Turk, the: the ruler of Ottoman Turkey at the time Machiavelli composed *The Prince* was Selim I, who overthrew the Mameluk regime of Egypt in 1517 and ruled between 1511 and 1520.

Valentino, Duke: *see* Borgia, Cesare.

Venafro, Antonio da: (d. 1459), one of the closest and most trusted of Pandolfo Petrucci's advisers in Siena.

Virgil: (70–19 BC), Publius Vergilius Maro, author of Rome's greatest epic poem, *The Aeneid*, about the founding of the city of Rome by descendants of Aeneas and other Trojan fugitives from the sack of Troy by the Greeks.

Visconti, Bernarbò: (1323–85), ruler of Milan and the province of Lombardy between 1355 and his death. Because of his disdain for his nephew Gian Galeazzo Visconti, who ruled in Pavia, Bernardo treated him contemptuously, but was captured by him, imprisoned, and probably murdered in prison in 1385.

Vitelli, Niccolò: (1414–86), mercenary soldier and ruler of Città di Castello (Umbria), a position he gained by murdering a number of the city's noblemen in 1468. After being driven out of the city in 1474, he returned in 1482. Four of his sons followed in his footsteps as mercenary soldiers, and all ended badly.

Vitelli, Paulo: (1465–99), son of Niccolò and a mercenary leader after being exiled from Città di Castello by Pope Innocent VIII in 1487 after his father's death. Although he gained a great reputation as a *condottiere* and was given command of Florentine forces in 1498 in a war waged against the city of Pisa, Paulo's actions seemed to indicate that he was betraying his employers. Arrested, he was beheaded in 1499.

Vitelli, Vitellozzo: (1470–1502), mercenary leader and son of Niccolò, who fought for Florence until the Florentines executed his brother Paulo for treason. Subsequently Vitellozzo served under Cesare Borgia, but after joining the conspiracy against Borgia that was hatched at Magione in 1502, Vitellozzo, Oliverotto of Fermo, and members of the Orsini family were tricked by Borgia at Senigallia. Vitellozzo was strangled with Oliverotto on the last day of 1502.

Xenophon: Athenian soldier and writer from the fifth century BC who accompanied the Greek army serving under Cyrus the Great against Artaxerxes. After the death of Cyrus Xenophon commanded the Greek soldiers in a famous retreat back home, recounted in his book the *Anabasis*. Xenophon's *Cyropaedia* is a fictional account of the education of Cyrus, and is one of the earliest and most celebrated treatises about the training a ruler ought to receive. Such a work was of obvious interest to Machiavelli.

INDEX

Note. The Index covers only the text of *The Prince*. For proper names and historical figures, see Glossary of Proper Names.

American Literature

British and Irish Literature

Children's Literature

Classics and Ancient Literature

Colonial Literature

Eastern Literature

European Literature

Gothic Literature

History

Medieval Literature

Oxford English Drama

Poetry

Philosophy

Politics

Religion

The Oxford Shakespeare

A complete list of Oxford World's Classics, including Authors in Context, Oxford English Drama, and the Oxford Shakespeare, is available in the UK from the Marketing Services Department, Oxford University Press, Great Clarendon Street, Oxford OX2 6DP, or visit the website at www.oup.com/uk/worldsclassics.

In the USA, visit www.oup.com/us/owc for a complete title list.

Oxford World's Classics are available from all good bookshops. In case of difficulty, customers in the UK should contact Oxford University Press Bookshop, 116 High Street, Oxford OX1 4BR.

Bhagavad Gita

The Bible Authorized King James Version
With Apocrypha

Dhammapada

Dharmasūtras

The Koran

The Pañcatantra

**The Sauptikaparvan (from the
Mahabharata)**

**The Tale of Sinuhe and Other Ancient
Egyptian Poems**

Upaniṣads

ANSELM OF CANTERBURY **The Major Works**

THOMAS AQUINAS **Selected Philosophical Writings**

AUGUSTINE **The Confessions**
On Christian Teaching

BEDE **The Ecclesiastical History**

HEMACANDRA **The Lives of the Jain Elders**

KĀLIDĀSA **The Recognition of Śakuntalā**

MANJHAN **Madhumalati**

ŚĀNTIDEVA **The Bodhicaryāvatāra**